THE
ROAD TO
VATICAN II

THE ROAD TO VATICAN II

Key Changes in Theology

Maureen Sullivan, OP

Paulist Press
New York/Mahwah, NJ

Cover design by Cynthia Dunne
Book design by Lynn Else

Library of Congress Cataloging-in-Publication Data
Sullivan, Maureen.
    The road to Vatican II : key changes in theology / Maureen Sullivan.
      p. cm.
    Includes bibliographical references and index.
    ISBN 978–0–8091–4277–4 (alk. paper)
    1. Vatican Council (2nd : 1962–1965) 2. Catholic Church—Doctrines. 3. Catholic Church—History—19th century. 4. Catholic Church—History—20th century. I. Title.
BX8301962.S9153 2007
262′.52—dc22

2006037762

Published by Paulist Press
997 Macarthur Boulevard
Mahwah, New Jersey 07430

www.paulistpress.com

Printed and bound in the
United States of America

CONTENTS

Contents

*"To contemplate and to give to others
the fruits of that contemplation."*

For my parents, who introduced me to the faith.

In memory of Yves Congar, OP, and M.-D. Chenu, OP,
my brothers in Saint Dominic,
who inspired me to search for the truth.

In gratitude to my congregation, the Dominican Sisters of Hope,
for giving me the opportunity to search for that truth.

ACKNOWLEDGMENTS

There is an old French proverb that states, "Gratitude is the memory of the heart." I understand this proverb better after having completed this book. Indeed, my heart is filled with memories of the many people who helped me to bring another story about Vatican II to life:

- My sisters, Patricia, Eileen, and Margaret, who listened patiently to my worries and wishes about the book.
- My friends, Gloria Cardita and Mary Feigen, OP, who never failed to encourage me.
- My congregation, the Dominican Sisters of Hope, who believed in the story I wanted to tell and supported me throughout the process. The "voice" of that support came frequently from my prioress, Catherine McDonnell, OP. Her humorous phone calls and e-mails kept me smiling and confident.
- The "angels" of Geisel Library at St. Anselm College: Judy Romein, Martha Dickerson, Madeleine Greiner, Sue Gagnon, and Laura Poppert. They gave of their expertise— and always with a smile. I am indebted to them for the help they gave me with my research.
- Denise Reagan and Linda Bradley, secretaries who constantly gave "above and beyond the call of duty."
- My colleagues in the theology department of St. Anselm College who encouraged me, expressed interest in my project, and gave advice along the way.
- My wonderful students at St. Anselm....I wonder if they will ever realize what a privilege it has been for me to introduce them to that grace-filled moment in the church—Vatican II.

- Gerald O'Collins, SJ, who has been the inspiration for anything I have ever written about the Second Vatican Council. He has been friend and theological advisor throughout my journey.
- Christopher Bellitto, PhD, my editor, my advice-giver, and—always—my friend. His careful reading of my chapters and his excellent advice are appreciated more than he could ever imagine.
- Finally, Pope John XXIII—a man of hope and an instrument of the Spirit. My life took a different turn because of him, and I will always be grateful.

These people have left their mark on my life and on this book. The credit belongs to them, the responsibility belongs to me. I hope I have done some justice to the ongoing story of Pope John's XXIII's great council.

INTRODUCTION

How does one tell the story of the Second Vatican Council? It is a question that has fascinated many people over the past forty years—challenged them as well, because, for one thing, more than one story is involved. Why was this council called, what did it hope to accomplish, what actually happened at the council, what impact did it have on Roman Catholicism, on the world at large? These are all legitimate questions—each with its own story. This book is an attempt to tell one such story.

October 11, 1962, was a magnificent sun-drenched day in Rome. Another moment in God's unfolding drama of salvation was about to occur. More than 2,500 bishops, representatives from all over the world, began their procession into St. Peter's Basilica. They were followed by a man who will be remembered in history for many reasons. One of those was about to unfold—the Second Vatican Council. At the end of that long procession was Pope John XXIII. One can only wonder what was in his mind that day as his council was about to begin.

I have often wished I could go back in time to that day, to have been a witness to this event. It has shaped the lives of so many and continues to do so today, four decades later. However, my years of study about Vatican II inspired me to go back in time even further—to before 1962. Why? When one studies the event known as the Second Vatican Council, one is struck by many things. One thing stands out for me: How is it possible that so much could have been accomplished in so short a time? After all, each of the four sessions of the council met for only a few months during the fall from 1962 to 1965. Yet, the bishops, who often disagreed on the most critical issues, managed to produce sixteen documents that touched the very essence of the Catholic faith. They produced a charter for the

1

twentieth-century church and beyond. And, in the forty years since then, Vatican II has spawned thousands of books, articles, conferences, and doctoral theses. The enormity of what the council fathers had achieved intrigued me and, I confess, became the inspiration for this book. I became fascinated with the story *behind* the story. I was always convinced that the Holy Spirit had been hard at work at the council. My research for this book demonstrated that the Spirit's work at Vatican II began long before 1962. And that is the story I wish to tell. I want to uncover some of those developments that took place on the road to Vatican II. I want to highlight those remarkable theologians whose efforts were the seeds of what would flourish at the council, those theologians who would ultimately be referred to as "the architects of Vatican II." What were their central ideas? How did they develop? How were they received during their time in history? What kinds of changes came about as a result of their theological inquiries? As Vatican II expert Joseph Komonchak has written:

> To know what Vatican II did and said one has to consult the sixteen documents which it produced, yes; but to give a sense of what Vatican II was as experienced and what it means as an event, the documents are inadequate. One has to turn to the people who helped make Vatican II what it was.[1]

Over the years, other theologians have offered wonderful insights in this regard. I hope I can add to what they have done.

This desire to look back in no way diminishes the incredible achievements of the council fathers. If anything, it demonstrates their openness to the Spirit working in and through them. It demonstrates their theological preparedness as well. The time is right to take a serious look at "the road to Vatican II."

A key question for me is this: How and why did Vatican II happen? For Catholics of a certain age today, their understanding of church is divided into two parts: before Vatican II and after Vatican II. I am one of those Catholics. I have lived in both churches and continue to maintain a love for both. The church before Vatican II was the church of my youth, of my journey into

Christianity—a journey filled with so many wonderful memories: rituals, processions, incense, lots of nuns. Maybe I remember it so fondly because, in truth, life did seem simpler then. Then I grew up and was introduced to an understanding of church that emerged from the Second Vatican Council. Had it not been for my own theological studies, I do not know that I would have been able to embrace it as warmly as I did. Perhaps, like many Catholics, I would have wondered, "What did you do to my church?" But precisely because of my work in theology, I welcomed this image of church. I love this image because it is the one that we find in the Christian community's earliest expression of being church: the New Testament.

I teach theology to undergraduate students at St. Anselm College in New Hampshire, and I thoroughly enjoy the opportunity of helping to prepare the twenty-first-century church. But it is quite a challenge to try to convey exactly what Vatican II was and why we make such a fuss about this event. After all, my students inherited the church after the council. They know no other image of church. Yet, I remain convinced that they need to have the "whole story," so to speak—they need to understand this amazing, grace-filled moment in the life of the Catholic community. Something truly Spirit-filled occurred in the life of the church. We were touched by grace, and what emerges from the teachings of Vatican II is a church with a human face, a church that stands humbly before its God, knowing that all is gift. I want my students to know how that happened.

Before I go on, perhaps a qualifying remark is needed. The church is the people of God—divinely founded and divinely guided, but in the hands of frail, wounded human beings for the past two thousand years. Where you have humans, you have the possibility for error, for sin, for evil. You also have the possibility for greatness, since each of us is a God-bearer. The point is this: The church is not perfect. Only God holds that esteemed attribute. So, in my enthusiasm for Vatican II, I do not want my readers to get the wrong impression. Not everything before Vatican II was bad. We have many saints, scholars, and witnesses to prove that point. And not every development after the council was for the betterment of the people of God. Still, I am convinced that the Second

Vatican Council was the work of the Spirit in our midst. And I hope to make a legitimate argument for this belief in the course of this book. I want to look at "the bumpy road of the century of theology" leading up to 1962…through the lens of the Holy Spirit, as it were, because the handprint of this Spirit is so very evident. Recently, one of the bishops who attended the council was asked who he thought was the most important figure at Vatican II. He said that most people would probably say it was John XXIII or Paul VI, but, in his mind, it was the Holy Spirit—whose presence was almost palpable.[2]

As we move through the chapters that follow, we examine the kinds of theological developments that occurred in Catholic thinking, especially in the area of ecclesiology (the study of the church); the shift from a hierarchical model of church to a *communio* model; the shift from a church suspicious of those outside the faith to a church eager to explore the path to Christian unity; a shift in the church's view of the outside world, from a church that viewed the world as alien to itself, an entity in dire need of salvation, to a church that saw the world as a partner in dialogue, recognizing the incarnational mystery at work in that world; a shift in the church's self-understanding, a church humbled by the reality that it is but an instrument of the kingdom and hence always in need of renewal and reform. For those of us fortunate enough to have lived in both churches—pre–Vatican II and post–Vatican II—and therefore able to see the difference, these were indeed major developments. How is it possible that such immense changes could occur in a church that had prided itself on the consistency, even immutability of its positions, since the Council of Trent in the sixteenth century?

The title of this book gives a hint regarding the answer to that question. A key point that is made throughout the book is this: In the years before the council, the approach to doing theology was primarily monolithic. I say *primarily* because, as I hope to show, there were those prophets among us who were attempting to do theology in a "new key." Their efforts, which bore fruit at the council and in the years since 1965, reflect a major change in theological method. Every academic discipline has its own method by which it achieves it goal. For example, in the sciences, the methodology used involves (at the risk of oversimplifying the great work done in the sciences!) three steps: an hypothesis, an experiment, and, finally, a judgment. Scientists begin with a "What if" question and then set out to prove their hypothesis. Theology must employ a very different methodology. Other disciplines set out to *search* for the truth; theology begins its work *with* the truth: the revelation of God given to us in the person of Jesus Christ. And, in the years prior to the council, the way we read scripture guided us in the theological process. It was in the very manner by which we read the scriptures that a remarkable development was beginning to emerge in the years before Vatican II, a development that would pave the way for new theological paradigms that would ultimately affect the way we would do theology in the future. Chapter 1 takes an in-depth look at these paradigm shifts, but first we must examine a theological development that would change the way we would read, interpret, and understand the word of God. Theologians refer to this as the "historical critical method."

This method is "a scientific technique which was developed in the 19th century for understanding written texts in their original setting."[3] It is usually associated with the efforts of biblical scholars to interpret and understand scripture.

> The language in which the text was written, the culture and times of the author, and the religious concerns of the people for whom it was originally written were now to be taken into account. (The biblical study methods that consider these elements are called "critical" approaches—not in the negative sense of "criticizing" but that of "looking carefully.")[4]

There are three basic approaches used in biblical criticism: (1) literary criticism, which looks at questions of authorship of a given book in the Bible as well as how the document came to be written; (2) form criticism, which seeks to determine the various literary genres or forms in the Bible—such as hymns, miracle stories, allegories; and (3) redaction criticism, which seeks to uncover the theological viewpoint of the biblical author—clearly seen in the Gospels of Mark, Matthew, Luke, and John. Each tells the Jesus story from a particular theological viewpoint.

For Catholics, the use of the historical critical method is a relatively recent development. Before Vatican II, the Bible played a limited role in the lives of most Catholics. For the most part, reading the Bible was viewed as a Protestant devotion.[5] This notion dates back to Martin Luther and the Protestant Reformation in the sixteenth century. Today, however, it would be rare to find a Catholic college that does not offer a course in the study of the Bible, and students are quite surprised to hear that such courses are, in fact, a post–Vatican II development.

The use of the historical critical method is indeed recent in Catholic biblical scholarship. The official door to a more critical reading of scripture was opened by Pope Pius XII on September 30, 1943, when he issued the encyclical *Divino Afflante Spiritu,* which favored a more scientific approach to reading the Bible instead of the fundamentalist and overly spiritual approach that prevailed at that time. Pius XII wrote:

> The interpreter must, as it were, go back wholly in spirit to those remote centuries of the East and with the aid of history, archaeology, ethnology, and other sciences accurately determine what modes of writing, so to speak, the authors of that ancient period would be likely to use and in fact did use.[6]

This was a remarkable moment for the study and interpretation of the Bible. The pope's encouragement to study the Bible in the original ancient languages and the realization that the truths of the Bible appeared in different literary forms were profoundly liberating for the biblical theologians at the time. Catholic biblical scholars became experts in the historical critical approach. Armed with the tools of biblical criticism, these theologians sought "to determine as accurately as possible what the text meant in its historical context."[7]

One cannot overestimate the significance of this development—not only for the interpretation of scripture but also for the countless areas in theology that would be affected by a new understanding of the word of God. As an example, let us take a look at a text from 1 Corinthians. In chapter 7, verses 25 and 32, Saint Paul is obviously responding to a question raised by the Corinthian community—whether it is better to remain a virgin or to marry. Saint Paul responds:

> Now, concerning virgins, I have no command of the Lord....I think that in view of the impending crisis, it is well for you to remain as you are....I want you to be free from anxieties. The unmarried man is anxious about the affairs of the Lord, how to please the Lord; but the married man is anxious about the affairs of the world...and his interests are divided.[8]

As we know, prior to the acceptance of the historical critical method, the Catholic Church read the Bible often without historical insight. So, we took Paul at his word and taught that a celibate life was superior to the married life. Now, let us reread Paul's response with the eyes of the historical critical method. Paul says, "In view of the impending crisis...." Using the new tools of biblical criticism, scholars came to understand what this text meant in its original context. When Paul speaks about the "impending crisis," he is referring to a common belief held at that time, a belief that the *parousia* (the end of the world) was imminent, and the risen Christ would return during their very lifetimes. So, 1 Corinthians 7, verses 25 and 32, is not a teaching on the superiority of celibacy in and of itself but rather a very practical piece of instruction from Paul. If the Lord is coming back soon, then remaining a virgin, being concerned with the affairs of the Lord, and concentrating on preparing oneself for the second coming makes sense. A new era in Catholic biblical scholarship had arrived.

The use of the historical critical method would have a tremendous impact on theology as a whole, not just the field of biblical studies. Once we began to legitimize the validity of history as a category to be included in the theological process, the results were enriching and liberating. We came to recognize that the church is affected by history, that all expressions of theological truth are conditioned by the time period in which they are expressed. For centuries, official Catholicism was marked by a static view of reality and resisted a historical, dynamic way of

understanding the world, denying even the possibility of any genuine development in religious thought. Since the Council of
Trent in the sixteenth century, even the word *reform* was to be
avoided.[9]

But one cannot limit the Spirit of God. And, it would seem
that the fathers at Vatican II understood this point. They produced
sixteen documents that reflected the extraordinary theological
developments that had emerged in the years before the council
even began. Indeed, the documents of the council did not occur in
a vacuum. In large part, they were the result of a "Copernican turn"
in the way we did theology. In addition to the emergence of the historical critical method, three major paradigm shifts had occurred in
the field of theology, shifts that would "change theology," paving
the road to Vatican II. These shifts are the topic of chapter 1. Then,
in the remaining chapters, we look at how the changing theology
was and is reflected in the church's attitude toward the world,
toward the laity, and toward its own self-understanding.

One comment should be made here. Contemporary theology
is very much aware of the need to use inclusive language. However,
this is a recent development. The reader will not find inclusive language in documents that were written in the 1960s, nor will it be
found in the writings of theologians in the years before we became
conscious of the need to employ inclusive language.

Throughout the book, I introduce you to some remarkable
people. We will meet some of the great ones: Johann Adam Mohler
(1796–1838), John Henry Newman (1801–90), Romano Guardini
(1885–1968), M.-D. Chenu, OP (1895–1990), Karl Rahner, SJ
(1904–84), Yves Congar, OP (1904–95), Henri de Lubac, SJ
(1925–74), and others. These names may not mean a great deal to
you at this point, but—if I am successful in the pages to come—you
will come to know them quite well. You may come to view them—
as I do—as the precursors of Vatican II, the architects of what
would become the theology of the Second Vatican Council. I hope
you will come to admire them as well because of what they have
achieved—often in the face of hardship. Many suffered the suspi-
cions and discipline of their own church during their day. They
were prophets among us, but—like the Old Testament prophets—
they were not always received very well.

It is their story that intrigues me. Who were they? What were their key theological ideas? How did they "change" theology? How did their ideas pave the road to Vatican II and ultimately find a home in the documents of Vatican II? What can contemporary theologians learn from them?

These great theologians have something else in common, something that is expressed so well in the following excerpt from a homily drafted by Bishop Kenneth Untener:

> We accomplish in our lifetime only a tiny fraction of the
>   magnificent enterprise that is God's work.
> Nothing we do is complete.
> No statement says all that could be said.
> We plant the seeds that will one day grow.
> We lay foundations that will need further development.
> We may never see the end results, but that is the differ-
>   ence between the master builder and the worker.
> We are the workers, not the master builder.
> We are ministers, not messiahs.
> We are prophets of a future not our own.

This prayer should be at the center of every theologian's work. The object of our study is divine mystery, and that reality should keep us humble.

1
THEOLOGY IN TRANSITION

Paradigm Shifts in Theology

It would appear that the task of a theologian is quite simple: to study the divine-human relationship and then articulate its meaning for others. Truth be told, it is not all that simple. Good theology requires a sound methodology, and a study of how theology has evolved over the years demonstrates two things: first, the importance of methodology for the theological process and, second, the many changes in the methodology employed.

Theological method begins with certain philosophical presuppositions. In the century or so before Vatican II, these presuppositions were drawn primarily from the medieval philosophy of the Scholastics. Nineteenth-century proponents of this approach, known as "neoscholasticism," held certain beliefs in common. For one thing, they shared a general ignorance of the historical critical method. They also held a basic disdain for the conclusions of modern science. However, alongside these theologians were those who were moving away from neoscholasticism and biblical fundamentalism. These new theologians were greatly influenced by three paradigm shifts that would bring about an immense change in the way we would do theology. The theological process was undergoing a significant transition, and transitions are rarely easy. They can produce great anxiety and hesitation, especially for a church that had prided itself on its immutability, on the unchanging nature of its teachings. The struggle would involve breaking away from previous ways of thinking without sacrificing the core of the faith or fidelity to the church.[1]

As we study the research in this area, one point begins to become clear:

It was not Vatican II that brought about the revolutionary changes in the church: a totally new approach to human and Christian existences brought about Vatican II. Popes, bishops, theologians were just instruments of a moving force which must be found within the whole human experience, sharing in God's providential presence in the world.[2]

How else to explain the sequence of events? How else to explain the election of Angelo Roncalli after the powerful papacy of Pope Pius XII? We have been told that the cardinals were having difficulty agreeing on who would succeed Pius XII and that they decided to go with Roncalli, thinking he would be a good "interim" pope. It would seem that the Spirit of God had other plans for Roncalli, who, only three months into his papacy, would issue the call for an ecumenical council.

Clearly, something very significant was happening in the world of theology. We can point to three major shifts that occurred in the years leading up to Vatican II, three paradigm shifts that would have a critical impact on the theological enterprise. First, theologians speak about a shift from a classicist worldview to a historically conscious worldview. A *worldview* is the way we perceive reality. The traditional classicist view maintained the truth of the past as certain and unchangeable for every future time and culture. The historically conscious worldview holds that every expression of a theological truth is historically conditioned, a product of the time period in which it is expressed. This does not mean that the basic truths of the faith change. Rather, believers come to deeper insights into those truths and how they illuminate and are illuminated by contemporary conditions. John XXIII espoused this position in his opening address at the council when he distinguished the ancient deposit of faith in itself from the ways that the faith is expressed for every generation.[3] Implied in this comment is that each new age presents new data, new questions, new discoveries that theologians must think about when they seek to give reasons for the hope that is in them.

A *second* shift was in the area of methodology. In the years before the council, the primary methodology was referred to as "deductive." The basic task of theology has always been to study the divine-human relationship, and in the deductive approach, theologians began their investigations with the divine partner. I am oversimplifying here. But theologians took their "picture" of God from the scriptures, and then they came across such lines in scripture as "Be perfect, therefore, as your heavenly Father is perfect."[4] And, since at that time we read the Bible nonhistorically, the theological enterprise assumed that was how humans should act. This expectation of divine behavior from nondivine beings (quite prevalent in pre–Vatican II thinking) caused much frustration and guilt for those Catholics who came to realize the impossibility of such an expectation. This approach did not take the human condition into consideration as a genuine source of truth in the doing of theology. But theologians were coming to the realization that if they want the gospel to take root in the hearts and souls of humans, they must understand the needs and desires of the human person.

The council fathers realized this as well. If the church is to be in dialogue with the people of God, it must take seriously the world in which these people live. The council fathers' awareness of this need results from the shift from a more or less exclusively deductive methodology to allow for an inductive methodology that focuses on the human person as a source of truth in the theological process. In the nineteenth century, John Henry Newman

> took upon himself the task of introducing the inductive temper of [that century] into Christian theology. It is his concern for the "real" or the "whole" man that makes him so outstanding [in his time]. For him...theology is a search for the meaning of man saved, rather than an abstract definition of God who saves man.[5]

In this methodology, the reality of the human condition—with all its strengths and limitations—becomes a factor in the doing of theology. Perhaps the best example of inductive methodology in the council documents is found in *Gaudium et Spes*. The very first line of the document reads:

> The joys and the hopes, the griefs and the anxieties of the followers of Christ...indeed, nothing genuinely

> human fails to raise an echo in their hearts....Therefore
> the Council focuses its attention on the world of men,
> the whole human family along with the sum of those
> realities in the midst of which that family lives.[6]

For those of us introduced to the church before Vatican II, this opening line is astonishing. *Gaudium et Spes* clearly departs from the pre–Vatican II deductive methodology, which probably would have opened with an abstract statement about the church. Rather, we find here a perfect example of the inductive methodology that begins in the concrete, in the real world of men and women, taking the human condition very seriously in its theologizing. Only in this way can the gospel have real meaning, only then can this message take root. How else can faith truly touch the human person?

It should be noted here that there were those in the church (today as well) who were not pleased with this shift. In their minds, beginning with the human condition, with human experience, somehow prepared the way for a kind of relativism, or the view that truth changes with changes in cultures and societies and varies from individual to individual. You have your truth, I have my truth. In fact, there does exist such a possibility, should the inductive approach be used incorrectly. But the proponents of inductive methodology believed there was a safeguard against relativism. That safeguard was the very gospel itself. The theology that emerges from an inductive methodology is one that takes human experience seriously and values it as a source of genuine truth. Inductive theologians analyze the human mind and discover its transcendent capacity. We are the only species that can go beyond the empirical and raise questions about the "other world." Inductive theologians have found that in their study of the human person, questions about God "naturally" arise.

The *third* shift that would have a significant impact on the way we do theology came in the way we taught the faith. We might label this the move from the "apologetic" approach to the "foundational" approach in teaching the faith. In the field of theology, the word *apology* does not mean "I am sorry." Rather, it describes the way we taught. The earliest theologians (second and third centuries) have frequently been called "apologists." They were the defenders of the faith at a time when many heresies were occurring and hostile "outsiders" were persecuting Christians. The apologists' task was not so much to explain the faith but to state the faith. So an apologetic approach to teaching is one that focuses on stating and defending truths of the faith, often at the neglect of explaining what they might mean.

Anyone who received religious education prior to Vatican II would have experienced the apologetic approach in the *Baltimore Catechism*. Good as it was on many levels, this catechism focused more on saying what the truths of the faith were and less on what those truths might mean in our everyday lives. And, given the world as we knew it in the 1950s, that approach worked very well. We did not question our parents, our police officers, or—heaven forbid—our religious leaders. We simply accepted the truths as given. But the 1960s ushered in a new way of thinking. What might have worked in the 1950s—something is right because an authority figure said it was right—was no longer viable. The 1960s brought about the "What does it mean?" generation. Now the task of theologians was not simply to reiterate the truths of the faith. No, now their task was to provide the foundation for the faith. As theologian Monica Hellwig has stated:

> The questions of all past generations are still with us in some form, but the answers will never have the same appearance of absolute certainty or unshakeable permanence. We must still be prepared for the doubts of the thoughtful and committed believer....It is necessary to establish the rationality of our endeavor.[7]

Hence, we speak of the shift from the apologetic approach to the foundational approach in our efforts to evangelize a new generation. Sometimes when I am teaching this concept, I explain the apologetic approach as the "I'm the mommy" approach—something is right because I said it was right. Parents know that children reach a point where that no longer suffices; the child wants to know why. And that is what happened to the people of God: they reached a point where they wanted to know why. And, in the years leading up to the Second Vatican Council, we find a good number of theologians whose theology clearly demonstrated the impact of these shifts in theology.

The Task of the Theologian

To be a theologian is a great privilege: the object of our study is God, the divine mystery. There are, however, some misconceptions about the task of a theologian. Dominican Aidan Nichols has singled out three such misconceptions. They are worth noting here because they can serve as an important backdrop to our discussion of those theologians who "changed theology" and paved the road to Vatican II.

First, there are those who would "dismiss the rational claims of theology" because the mysteries of the Christian religion transcend the ability of the finite human person. Why bother trying to understand these mysteries? This position would claim that it is possible to have a spirituality but not a theology...that grace can change the heart but not the mind.

A second misconception would hold that the task of a theologian is to acquire a great deal of information about the Bible and the church. In this view, theologians become "professional rememberers."

A third misconception views the theologian as someone whose task is simply to repeat the official teachings of the Magisterium. However, as Nichols points out, though theologians do have the responsibility to defend the teachings of the church, theology has a much wider task. That task is to "explore the riches of this shared faith by putting ever-new questions to it and about it." Nichols then offers a very rich definition of theology—it is "the disciplined exploration of Revelation."[8]

As was noted earlier, theology differs from other academic disciplines in an important way. Most fields of study are on a quest to *find* the truth. Theology begins *with* the truth: revelation. We believe that God has revealed the truth, and so our task is a quest to *understand* the truth that has been given to us: God, revealed in the person of Jesus Christ. And this quest is disciplined in that we are not free to say anything we want to say; we are bound by scripture and tradition. But this quest is also an exploration. Theology is not simply a proclamation of something that is obvious to all believers. Rather, theology brings questions to bear on the Christian story in order to better understand it. It searches for deeper insights and attempts to articulate the good news for each new generation, to find ways for the story to take root in the everyday lives of believers.

The New Theology

Indeed, something very significant was happening in the field of theology in the century before Vatican II. In those years, we find some scholars (primarily European) who were approaching theology in a very different manner. Their approach was called *nouvelle theologie* (the "new theology") and was viewed by many as a threat to the neoscholasticism that was prevalent in the late nineteenth and early twentieth centuries.[9] It should be noted that neoscholasticism was—for the most part—the preferred approach of the official teachers in the church, the Magisterium. Because of this perceived threat, most of the theologians in this new group were censored by the Vatican. In 1950, Pope Pius XII issued *Humani Generis* (Of the Human Race), an encyclical that rejected the new theology and required Catholic scholars to return to the orthodoxy provided by Scholasticism. This was a painful time for those involved in the theological process. Interestingly enough, "although almost all the new theologians were silenced by Pope Pius XII, they were all not only eventually rehabilitated, but many were to become the true architects of the Vatican II documents."[10] Theologians such as Yves Congar, OP, M.-D. Chenu, OP, and Henri de Lubac, SJ, were among those labeled as members of the new theology. We find that they had certain theological preferences in common: a genuine commitment to historical and critical methodology, a disenchantment with Scholasticism, a desire to return to the Bible and the patristic time period for theological guidance, an openness to ecumenical dialogue, and an appreciation for the concept of ongoing revelation—the idea that while the basic truths of the faith do not change or increase, God continues to speak to us (through the liv-

17

ing words of the scriptures, worship, the signs of the times, and in many other ways). Thus, our insights into and understanding of revealed truths develop over time.

Let us now take a more focused look at some of these theologians and their ideas. We will meet them again in later chapters as we discover the imprint of their theology in the teachings of the Second Vatican Council.

The New Theologians

Yves Congar, OP (1904–95)

The new theologians made a remarkable contribution in numerous areas of theology. Yves Congar, OP, was among the most important of these contributors. One thing becomes very clear in all that has been written by Congar and by others who have written about him: He loved his church and dedicated his life to articulating the mystery of that church to others.

After the first session of Vatican II, in December 1962, Congar wrote:

> It [the Council] is a spirit of frankness and freedom, free from all servility and self-seeking intrigue; it is at the service of mankind, seeking neither power nor privilege; it is evangelical and apostolic, a spirit of reverence and love for all men; it is open-minded toward others and has dropped any suggestion of scoring theological or clerical points. Lastly, it is a sustained attentiveness to hear what God, who does speak through events, is asking from his church today.[11]

The reader is struck by Congar's enthusiasm for what he observed after only three months at the council. However, a look at what he had been writing about in the decades before Vatican II helps to explain his enthusiasm, for these were precisely the kinds of developments he had been suggesting. As Joseph Komonchak has stated, "In few people is the quality of the council as a turning point more completely embodied than in Yves Congar."[12]

One of Congar's main contributions was "to stress an historically dynamic vision of church open to change."[13] This vision was, of course, in stark contrast to the prevailing vision of church before the council. In the minds of many during those years, the concept of change was viewed in a very negative light—as though change implied mistakes. Congar, on the other hand, saw change as something quite positive. Like so many theologians of *nouvelle theologie*, he understood the church as a mystery—divinely founded, but in the hands of humans. And, just as humans grow and develop, so too the human organism called "church" must do the same, remaining always attentive to the presence of God's Spirit in its midst.

But Congar's vision cost him dearly in the years before Vatican II. In his book, *Dialogue between Christians*, he wrote, "From the beginning of 1947 to the end of 1956, I knew nothing from that quarter (the Vatican) but an uninterrupted series of denunciations, warnings, restrictive or discriminatory measures and mistrustful interventions."[14]

One wonders how this "prophet" continued to be hopeful during this time. According to one commentator, "His patience... was rooted in the conviction that God is in charge and accomplishes his gracious design through us. For Congar, patience was always linked to the Cross....The Cross is the condition for every holy work."[15]

When one becomes aware of the ecclesial issues closest to Congar's heart, one can understand why Rome was uneasy with his ideas. As he looked forward to the beginning of the council, he wrote about three concepts he hoped would be addressed: new circumstances in ecumenical relations, more emphasis on the church (as opposed to a one-sided focus on the papacy), and the collegial authority of the bishops and the primacy of the pope.[16]

He hoped the council fathers would take a serious look at these concerns because his entire theological journey had been bound to them. However, as history has shown us, critique in the church has rarely been welcomed. We could cite many examples of the church's displeasure over criticism. One such example occurred in 1846. A theologian named Antonio Rosmini had written a book entitled *The Five Wounds of the Church*, in which he gave an account of the wounds that plagued the nineteenth-century church. It was published on the eve of the election of Pope Pius IX and was quickly placed on the Index of Forbidden Books.[17] Congar and his colleagues knew only too well the church's history in this regard. Clearly, "prophets are not without honor except in their own country."[18]

Still, Congar was committed to the movement of *ressourcement* (a return to the sources in the scripture and tradition), which uncovered an ecclesiology that was open to conversion and reform. The ecclesiology of the First Vatican Council (1869–70) had emphasized the church as institution, one that was an unchanging, fixed reality.[19] But, before and after 1870, theologians were at work rethinking the church's self-understanding, and were to benefit from the work of biblical scholars who focused on the church as the body of Christ and the people of God.

M.-D. Chenu, OP (1895–1990)

M.-D. Chenu, OP, is another French Dominican who played a pivotal role in the *nouvelle theologie*. His plea for the historical method in theology resulted in one of his books being placed on the Index (of Forbidden Books) in 1937. He was clearly among the most important forerunners of Vatican II. Chenu and his colleagues in the French church revitalized French Catholicism, and their efforts would come to fruition at the Second Vatican Council.

We spoke earlier about the shift from deductive to inductive methodology. In this regard, Chenu was truly a forerunner. Incarnation theology, which holds that as a result of the divine entering the human condition in the person of Jesus of Nazareth, the power and presence of God can act in and through created realities, is an integral part of the inductive method, and we see this clearly in Chenu's theology. One of the unfortunate features of the pre–Vatican II church was its self-imposed separation from the world in which it lived. Chenu's incarnational theology saw the error of this thinking.

Chenu was indeed a theological pioneer. Long before the inductive approach became "fashionable," he maintained,

> The life of the church is the first object of the theologian....To do theology is to be present to the revelation

given in the present life of the church and the present experience of Christendom....The theologian keeps his eyes upon Christendom in travail. This is how he is present to his time.[20]

The meaning of these words written in the 1930s, though foreign and disturbing to many in the church at the time, would find a home years later in Vatican II's Constitution on the Church in the Modern World, *Gaudium et Spes*.

Henri de Lubac, SJ (1925–74)

Contemporary theologian Joseph Komonchak has written extensively on events leading up to the Second Vatican Council. In an article on theology and culture in the middle of the twentieth century, he offers important insights, especially with regard to one of the "new theologians"—Henri de Lubac, SJ. According to Komonchak, the "new theology" was an attempt to bring the theological enterprise back from its self-imposed exile—and, "if a single work was considered to typify the 'new theology,' it was (Henri) de Lubac's *Surnaturel*."[21]

The relationship between nature and grace has always been central in theological discourse. According to de Lubac, nature is made for the supernatural. We may distinguish nature from grace, but must always remember that "mere" nature has never existed. The free gift and call of grace to communion with the life of God has always been there. Simply put, the dynamism of the human spirit remains unsatisfied without the vision of God.[22]

Clearly, one of the central goals of de Lubac and the other *ressourcement* thinkers was to bring about a contact between Catholic theology and contemporary thought. De Lubac, along with other thinkers of his day, recognized that *ressourcement* was not simply a return to forms and customs of the past but a return in the sense that "the life which gave birth to the church must spring up ever more vigorously without endangering her own proper and unalterable nature."[23] His countryman, Yves Congar agreed: "We have had to be faithful to the principles in depth, and so be unfaithful to the forms which it has taken on the surface."[24]

De Lubac's inquiries were grounded in an accurate exegesis of scripture and a serious study of the early church fathers. He also provided an openness to those outside the Roman Catholic faith with an approach to the supernatural that underlies all religion and affects all human existence.[25]

The Catholic Tübingen School of Theology

The way we do theology, theological method, is a focal point of this book, and the quest for an adequate method has a long history in Roman Catholic theology. The founding of the Catholic Tübingen School in Germany in the nineteenth century marks a critical turning point in this regard. This school was established in 1817 in Tübingen.

Johann Sebastian von Drey (1777–1853) is the founder of the Tübingen School, and many of Germany's most influential theologians were to be associated with Tübingen. Von Drey was largely responsible "for making history a constitutive component of theological method."[26] For the Tübingen theologians, "history is the organic growth and outworking of the Divine Spirit's self-expression. That is, history reveals an all-inclusive purpose, God's eternal design manifesting itself in time."[27] Hence, history moves toward the realization of God's kingdom, and this carries significant implications for a theology of church. Vatican II would make this concept one of its central themes, most notably in its designation of the church as the "pilgrim people of God." To be a pilgrim is to be on the way to a destination. The council's use of this concept would challenge the way the church understood itself in the past.

Johann Adam Mohler (1796–1838)

Johann Adam Mohler was one of Tübingen's best-known representatives, and he became a pivotal figure in the Catholic theological renewal of the twentieth century. A distinguishing characteristic of Mohler's theology is that he begins with the presence of the Holy Spirit in the Christian community. (The significance of this will become all too evident when we discuss the idea of a *communio* ecclesiology in chapter 4.) For Mohler, "the church is the external, visible form of a holy, living power of love which the Holy Spirit imparts."[28]

Such a belief would become the inspiration of many later theologians in their efforts to understand the church as mystery, that is, an entity that is both human and divine, institutional and mystical. Indeed, Mohler "bequeathed to modern Catholicism a conception of church that avoided the extremes of both the static and juridical notions of the Counter Reformation as well as the dominantly mystical and purely spiritual conception of an invisible church."[29]

Johann Adam Mohler is remembered in the history of ecclesiology for a number of significant contributions, ideas that future theologians would build upon. Three should be noted here: first, an early Spirit-centered view of church—largely forgotten in the nineteenth century—would have a huge impact on the twentieth century, especially on the thought of Yves Congar. Second, Mohler's incarnation-centered view of the church would be recovered in the thought of Yves Congar, the image of the mystical body of Christ. Its effects would be seen in Pope Pius XII's *Mystici Corporis* (Of the Mystical [Body] of Christ, 1943). Third, and most important, his blend of Christology and theological anthropology would ultimately affect the way that subsequent theologians would perceive the church.[30]

The theologians associated with the Tübingen School also made an enormous contribution to the way tradition was understood. For them, the ancient deposit of the faith was not to be understood as a fixed collection of truths, teachings, and practices, passed on like a fixed packet from one generation to another. Rather, they saw the deposit of faith as a living gospel. This represented a critical shift "from thinking of tradition as *tradita*, a content handed down from age to age, to *traditio*, an active transmission which is part of the living reality of the church."[31]

After 1840, the Tübingen School found itself in conflict with the revival of neoscholasticism that was supported by the official Roman Catholic Church. However, the efforts of some German and French theologians in the 1940s created a renewed interest. The hallmarks of Tübingen theology—its theology of revelation, its understanding of the development of doctrine and the role of the Holy Spirit in the church—will be revisited in later chapters.

23

John Henry Newman (1801–90)

In an introduction to a book on John Henry Newman,[32] theologian Gregory Baum aptly describes two mentalities that clashed at the Second Vatican Council. He refers to the minority bishops as "dogmatic," those who understood the church in a static manner. He then speaks about the majority bishops, calling them "historical," those who preferred to see the church as the incarnation of God's redemptive design. This group would understand the church in a dynamic fashion and favor reform and adaptation. Baum goes on to say that during Newman's time, these two mentalities were already at odds in the church. This conflict, still with us even today, "was rehearsed in the nineteenth century by Newman in his conflict with the ecclesiastical establishment."[33]

This fact, by itself, does not warrant our inclusion of Newman in the list of theological precursors to Vatican II—there are other more substantial reasons. Vatican II is sometimes referred to as "the Council of John Henry Newman."[34] And, during a papal audience in 1975, Pope Paul VI declared that Vatican II could be considered "Newman's hour."[35] One leading expert on Newman has noted that even though it might be difficult to locate Newman's direct influence in the documents of Vatican II, "there is no doubt that Vatican II upheld and vindicated those controversial positions that he espoused in his own time, and so often at his own personal cost."[36]

To be fair, not all theologians agree on Newman's connection to Vatican II. However, given all that has been written about Newman and his theology, I submit that Newman can be included in the long line of theologians leading up to the Second Vatican Council. An overview of some of Newman's key theological positions might convince the reader of this claim.

Newman began his theological career as a member of the Anglican Church in England, but in 1845 he converted to Catholicism. Newman was committed to many theological issues—among them "the inviolability of conscience, the dignity of the laity, and the freedom of theological investigation."[37] Many of the theological issues discussed at Vatican II were treated by Newman in his day: the question of ecumenism, the church-world relationship, the development of doctrine, the question of infallibility, faith and revelation. And, one of Newman's best known essays, *On Consulting the Faithful in Matters of Doctrine*, is often acknowledged as an anticipation of Vatican II.[38] As we see in chapter 4, Newman's thoughts in this regard found a home in the Dogmatic Constitution on the Church, *Lumen Gentium*.

Newman was clearly more in accord with the Tübingen School of Theology than with neoscholasticism.[39] He believed that a valid test of doctrine was not about immutability or antiquity, but about life and growth.[40] In his well-known *Essay on the Development of Doctrine*, he wrote, "From the nature of the human mind (we must take the view that) time is necessary for the full comprehension and perfection of great ideas....This may be called 'The Theory of the Development of Doctrine.'"[41]

This line of thinking is closely aligned with that of the Tübingen theologians, who believed that the church is an entity in the process of development. Indeed, for these theologians, the revelation of God is continually at work in the community; it unfolds throughout history.[42] Newman would agree "that doctrine does develop as the Holy Spirit assists the church to grasp the truth implicit in the apostolic deposit."[43] For a great idea to be understood, Newman was convinced that "it must change, in order to remain the same."[44] Newman continues, "In a higher world, it would be otherwise, but here below to live is to change, and to be perfect is to have changed often."[45] By the end of the nineteenth century, this concept of the development of doctrine, so central to Newman's theology, was widely accepted by the Catholic Church.

Earlier in this chapter, we talked about certain paradigm shifts that had a decisive impact on the way we do theology. The shift in methodology from deductive to inductive was discussed. Here again, we find a connection between John Henry Newman and the Tübingen theologians.

Newman's *Grammar of Assent* was published in 1870. In this work, Newman exhibits his "distrust of deductive reason....(He) begins not with universal propositions but with concrete experiences in which the whole person is involved."[46] Nearly one hundred years after Newman's work, Vatican II will give evidence of this approach in its documents, especially in the Pastoral Constitution on the Church in the Modern World, *Gaudium et Spes*.

Newman did not envision God simply as an "idea," a "concept." Instead, for him God was a concrete reality that man encounters in the consciousness of his own human situation.[47] This awareness of God as the very ground of our being is a foundational principle for inductive methodology. And, according to the Tübingen theologians, "Since the entire world is grounded in God, man becomes aware of God as he becomes aware of himself—our being is uniquely determined by our primal consciousness of the Other, of God."[48] Indeed, Newman and the members of the Tübingen School were prophets among us in their understanding of how the human person encounters God.

Before we move on to our next Vatican II precursor, two additional theological contributions of John Henry Newman warrant our attention: his understanding of infallibility (both how it pertains to the papacy and to the laity) and his teaching on the role of the laity in the mission of the church.

It was at the First Vatican Council (1869–70) that the church's teaching on infallibility was first officially articulated. Newman did not view this as a positive development. For one thing, he felt that the teaching needed more discussion to complete it, but Vatican I itself was never "officially" completed because of political turmoil in Rome. Also, he was fearful that, left as it was, the teaching could encourage a pope to act without consulting his brother bishops.[49] Still, his advice at the time to others who shared his concern was, "Let us be patient, let us have faith, and a new pope, and a reassembled council may trim the boat."[50] His prophetic words would eventually be fulfilled at Vatican II. Its treatment of the concept of infallibility included the role of the bishops.

Newman also paved the way for the Second Vatican Council in his understanding of the role of the laity in the mission of the church. His position, though controversial in his own day, would finally be accepted at Vatican II, particularly in *Lumen Gentium*, the Dogmatic Constitution on the Church. Newman held that all believers receive the Spirit of Truth at baptism. Today, theology speaks about the *sensus fidelium* (the "sense of the faithful"). It refers to the fact that the Holy Spirit is active in the whole church. Hence, the church's teaching emerges out of the entire church and is evidence of a mutuality between hierarchical authority and the faithful in the formulation of doctrine. But during his time, Newman was troubled with the failure of church leaders who did not appreciate the genuine role of the layperson in the church. No doubt, it was this concern that prompted a well-known comment to his own bishop "that the church would look foolish without the laity."[51] Surely, Newman would have been delighted to read Vatican II's Decree on the Apostolate of the Laity.

There is another element in Newman's theology of the laity that should be noted. One of the problems plaguing the church today is religious illiteracy. In the years since the council ended, we have not been as successful as we should have been in the area of religious education. There are any number of reasons to explain how this happened, but one thing does stand out. In our efforts to move away from the pre–Vatican II "Catechism style" of teaching—which was thought to be too juridical and legalistic and focused more on rote memory than understanding—we lost something along the way. I see it every day in my theology classes. So many students simply do not know the basic content of the faith. In Newman's day, it was not common for laypersons to become professional theologians, but he did maintain that all believers should receive a solid religious education. In his work, *The Present Position of Catholics in England*, he wrote:

> I want a laity, not arrogant, not rash in speech, not disputatious, but men who know their religion, who enter into it, who know just where they stand, who know what they hold, and what they do not, who know their creed so well, that they can give an account of it, who know so much of history that they can defend it.[52]

I think contemporary religious educators would heartily endorse these words of Newman.

Romano Guardini (1885–1968)

Our next theologian played a major role in the Catholic Church's ecclesiological journey into the twentieth century. Though born in Italy, Romano Guardini spent most of his life in Germany, emerging as one of Germany's most influential theologians; he stands out as one of the great forerunners of the Second Vatican Council. Indeed, one commentator claims, "In German-speaking lands there is no one who deserves more to be called a precursor of Vatican II."[53] Guardini's theological interests were many. He left his mark on the study of Christology, revelation, the inductive method, the attitude of the church toward the modern world, and—perhaps what he is best remembered for—the renewal of the liturgy.

At the heart of all of his theological endeavors is the person of Jesus Christ. The incarnation is one of the central mysteries of the Christian faith, and Christology is that branch of theology that inquires into this mystery—a mystery that holds that Jesus was both human and divine. Christology has two basic approaches: a Christology from above and a Christology from below. It is worth discussing the distinction between these approaches for two reasons: first, prior to the Second Vatican Council, there was a tendency in Catholic theology to emphasize Jesus' divine nature, often at the neglect of Jesus' human nature; second, an understanding of the distinction will enable us to better comprehend Guardini's Christology.

A Christology from above begins its discussion of the God-man with Jesus' divinity, with an acknowledgment of his preexistence as the second person of the Trinity. It then moves to the incarnation, God's unique entry into human history. An example of this Christology can be found in John's Gospel. His prologue begins with, "In the beginning was the Word, and the Word was with God and the Word was God."[54] On the other hand, the Gospels of Matthew, Mark, and Luke employ a (largely but not exclusively) Christology from below. They tell the story of the human Jesus, above all in his ministry, and move toward his divinity with the resurrection. Neither of these approaches is superior to the other—as long as both natures are acknowledged.

In his theology, which was fully Christocentric, Romano Guardini opted for a Christology from above. For Guardini, Jesus Christ is God's Word who has become flesh (John 1:14). In 1937, one of Guardini's best-known books, *The Lord*, was published. It contains a number of themes that are at the center of his Christology: Jesus Christ, the revealer of God; Jesus Christ as absolutely unique; the humanity of Jesus Christ; and Christian conversion. In his Christology, Guardini sought to communicate a living person, not merely information *about* this person.

Romano Guardini also left his mark on the way we understand revelation. Perhaps his major contribution, one that would be adopted at the Second Vatican Council, was his insistence that revelation was God's *personal* self-disclosure. As with his Christology, Guardini employs the language of person. This was in stark contrast to the prevailing view during his time, which perceived revelation more as a set of eternal truths, propositions about God, passed from generation to generation. This latter conception was the model of Vatican I and of neoscholasticism.

Two other points are worth noting regarding Guardini's theology of revelation: first, the importance of conversion—an authentic, human reception of God's personal self-disclosure results in our transformation...humans are changed when they receive love from another, how much more so when we truly receive God; second, Guardini emphasizes the role of the church as the witness to God's historical revelation.[55]

Earlier, we spoke about the shift that occurred from a deductive to an inductive methodology and how that changed the way we did theology. Here again, we find the mark of Romano Guardini.

In the years before the Second Vatican Council, it would be fair to say that theology did not take into account the individuality of cultures. For example, in our missionary endeavors, in our attempts to bring the good news to people around the world, we superimposed a Western, Eurocentric theology on local cultures. This would change, of course, with Vatican II's teaching on respect for various cultures and the need to inculturate the Christian message. However, long before the council, Guardini held that "a Christian view of the modern world must first of all understand a culture on its own terms."[56] This is inductive methodology at its best.

Related to this interest in the value of individual cultures is Guardini's stance on the modern world. For so many years, the church's attitude toward the world had been described as a "fortress mentality," the idea that the road to God somehow demanded an escape from modernity. Guardini came to believe that we would need to accept modernity with the hope of bringing the Christian witness to the world from within that world. In a letter written in 1925, Guardini claimed, "We must first say yes to our own age."[57]

Perhaps of all the theological interests of Guardini, he is best remembered for his contribution to the renewal of the liturgy. Ever since the 1600s, the Catholic Mass resembled a "performance." The priest performed the Mass and the faithful observed it. But Guardini believed in the active participation of the faithful at the celebration of the Eucharist. Of course, such participation is a challenge when the liturgy is conducted in a language that is foreign to most of the faithful. In 1966, looking back on the road to liturgical renewal, Guardini recalled that, "as a newly ordained priest, he hoped the day would come, when presiding at Mass, he would be able to say aloud in German, 'The Lord be with you.' Thanks to Vatican II, the day he had envisioned had arrived."[58]

Karl Rahner, SJ (1904–84)

Anyone who has ever traveled to a foreign country knows only too well the experience of utter relief when you come across someone who can be your translator. Catholic theology experienced a similar kind of relief with Karl Rahner, a Jesuit theologian who will probably be remembered as the most significant Catholic theologian of the twentieth century. Just as the language in a foreign country puzzles, frustrates, and confuses the tourist, the language of faith in the decades before Vatican II was producing similar effects in the Catholic faithful. We could say that a crisis of faith was beginning to emerge. We began to see a divorce between our "Sunday-go-to-church" life and our "rest-of-the-week" world. The traditional language of faith did not—perhaps could not—address this crisis. Rahner believed that modern men and women were living in a radically changed situation, one that called for theologians to find new ways to articulate Catholic theology. We needed a new language of faith.

Rahner offered three reasons for this crisis of faith. The first is pluralism. We no longer lived in a closed society, sharing the same faith or the same values. Second, the modern world was bringing an ever-growing body of knowledge to contemporary men and women, offering new data, raising new questions, suggesting a new understanding of history. Finally, Rahner pointed to what he called a "cal-cification" of theological concepts.[59] For so long, Catholic teaching about the faith had been based primarily on traditional statements made over the past fifteen hundred years. Such an approach could succeed in the past, but not now. Rahner insisted that theologians needed to find new ways to express the essential truths of the faith in a manner that would touch the hearts and lives of contemporary Christians in their everyday world. In this regard, Karl Rahner would emerge as the translator "par excellence."

Up until this point, the traditional Scholastic theology served as the language of faith. Rahner did not believe it could solve the crisis of faith. Anyone trained in religion prior to Vatican II would be very familiar with the traditional approach, the *Baltimore Catechism* serving as its primary tool. This catechism was published in 1885 and was used in religious education into the 1960s. As good as it was on certain levels, it contributed to what Rahner perceived as the crisis of faith. For one thing, learning about the faith was reduced to memorizing statements about the faith, leaving little room for genuine questions or healthy doubts. This approach also tended to proclaim the faith in the language of obligation. Rahner believed this kind of faith was the product of external indoctrination and learning by rote, resulting in little, if any, real understanding of the meaning of faith.[60]

Rahner knew the history of the church. He knew that ever since the Protestant Reformation in the sixteenth century, which resulted in the devastating rupture of Christian unity, the Roman Church often vigorously resisted new ideas. He knew the church was more and more isolated from modernity, sometimes even fearful of the world and the challenges it put to Christianity. But he also knew that the gospel needed to be preached in a way that would transform believers. In his book, *Foundations of Christian Faith*, Rahner wrote, "The effective mission of the church in the face of modern disbelief requires a testimony to the Christian message in which this message becomes intelligible for people today."[61] We look now to see how Rahner went about changing the language of faith.

Our examination of Rahner's theology makes clear that he epitomizes, perhaps more than any other theologian of his time, the fundamental paradigm shifts that changed the way we would do theology in the twenty-first century: from a classicist to an histori-cally conscious worldview, from an apologetic to a foundational style of teaching, and from a deductive to an inductive methodology.

We begin with his theological method, which is referred to as a transcendental, anthropological methodology. Theology is con-cerned with the divine-human relationship. The question of God, of course, is a critical one. Is there a God? Can we prove this God's existence? If yes, how do we come to know this God? What is this God like? Theologians have grappled with the question of God for centuries. In the past, the traditional arguments for God's existence seemed to be proving the existence of a being who is removed from the human condition, a being very distant from us, a being who is totally other. Rahner's method breaks away from the traditional approach. He begins his inquiry, not with God—but with the human person. Because Rahner is convinced that theology must be directed to the needs and questions of contemporary men and women, because theology must mediate the faith from within the context of their existence, the human person becomes the point of departure for Rahner. Hence, his method is *anthropological* because it begins with the human condition. It is *transcendent*, referring to humanity's dynamic orientation, its ability to transcend—to go beyond the empirical world toward communion with God.

In his examination of the human condition, Rahner discovers certain elements that are common to all humans. They are consti-tutive of what it means to be human. For one thing, humans are generally open to everything. By this openness, Rahner means that nothing in our world ever completely satisfies or fulfills us. We have a longing for perfect joy, perfect justice, fullness of knowledge and unconditional love—and yet we come to realize that such desires cannot be fulfilled here on earth. So, why do we have these desires? Is it just a defect in our nature, that all humans desire something that this world is incapable of giving? Or, is there another possible answer? For Rahner, and for all theologians who espouse this theological method, there is another possibility. The answer is God—the only one who can fulfill and complete the human longing.

In this regard, Rahner speaks about the "Supernatural Existential." The term *existential* is not a thing—it is a concept that

Rahner uses to explain a constitutive element in the human person. It is given to all humans by God at the moment of their creation, and it is utterly gratuitous (supernatural). This existential affects my whole being and is understood by Rahner as "the gift of being open to, even pining for, the divine source of meaning and fulfillment."[62] This concept carries significant theological implications for our understanding of grace, for the possibility of salvation for those outside the Christian Church, for the study of Christology and for making the Christian story more credible for contemporary men and women.

It should be noted here that even though Rahner's theology begins with an examination of the human condition, he is not simply reducing theology to human experience. In other words, he will not encourage a purely subjective understanding of Christian faith—to a deadly relativism. This is because humanity's transcendent nature, with its radical openness, points to what Rahner calls "the holy mystery"—God. It is this holy mystery who is at the center of Rahner's theology. It is this God that we encounter when we understand what it means to be human. For Rahner, "man's experience of himself is always an experience of God."[63] Hence, grace is quite simply the presence of God in the human person.

With regard to his treatment of the concept of grace, Rahner again departs from the traditional approach. In the past, theologians viewed human nature and grace as two separate entities. In this approach, grace comes across as something "added on" to nature, superimposed like icing on a cake. It became objectified, as though one could fill up one's soul with grace. Rahner insisted that human nature has never been without grace, that the presence of God in the very core of one's being constitutes the essence of the human condition. For this reason, rather than speak about "grace and nature," Rahner prefers to speak about a "graced nature."

The incarnation of God in the person of Jesus Christ is at the very center of Rahner's theology. The incarnation means, among other things, that the power of God is present in and can work through visible created realities. "For the believer, the history of the world is the history of grace."[64] In Jesus Christ, human persons find the satisfaction they have been seeking, which is why Rahner calls Christ "the absolute bringer of salvation."[65] Rahner insisted that there must be something in the human condition that enables humans to understand the resurrection as a fulfillment of their hopes and expectations. His inductive method found three elements that make the Christ story more credible to contemporary men and women: it speaks to the love of one's neighbor, to the phenomenon of death, and to humanity's inherent capacity for hope.[66] Or, as theologian Walter Kasper has written, "Jesus' life ended in a final openness. His history and his fate remain a question to which only God can give an answer."[67] Hence, for Rahner, Jesus is the ultimate revealer of God as well as the ultimate example of humanity's response to God.

Because inductive methodology is so central to Rahner's theology, more attention has been given to this paradigm shift. But Rahner is also an excellent example of the shift from apologetic to foundational teaching as well as the shift from the classicist to the historically conscious worldview. The very title of his best-known book, *Foundations of the Faith: An Introduction to the Idea of Christianity*, attests to Rahner's desire to provide contemporary believers with an understanding of the faith. He became convinced that the argument from authority, that something is true because an authority figure said it was true, no longer met the needs of modern men and women. He insisted that, in the face of modern disbelief, what was required was a testimony to the gospel that would be intelligible for contemporary believers and nonbelievers.

Rahner was also committed to an historically conscious worldview. The truths of revelation were revealed in the person of Jesus Christ, but each generation must explore these truths, come to a deeper understanding of them, and articulate them in a way that is both intelligible and credible. New situations, which bring new questions, require a new language to express the Christian story. Rahner believed this was a theologian's most important task—to be a "translator" for the people of God in each new generation.

It should be noted that, like so many theologians before him, over the years Rahner found himself the object of suspicion from the Roman Curia. But his vindication would come at Vatican II. He was called to serve as a *peritus*, a theological expert, at the council. In the chapters to follow, we will discover the strong influence of Rahner in the documents of the Second Vatican Council.

We spoke earlier about the prophetic quality of the theologians who paved the way to Vatican II. Among other things, a prophet can express the experience of God for others. Surely, Rahner was able to do this. His theological anthropology looked to the universal experience shared by all humans and found at the very center of this experience the presence of the holy mystery. His reflections were "always in the service of human hearts that had been addressed in time by grace."[68]

Conclusion

The years between the First Vatican Council (1869–70) and the Second Vatican Council, almost one hundred years later, produced a major change in the way we did theology. This chapter has been an attempt to provide an understanding into how theology changed, why it changed, and who was responsible for those changes that would ultimately pave the road to Vatican II.

The theologians discussed in this chapter were, of course, not the only ones involved in the process—but they are pivotal figures. And, they shared a number of things in common. They were convinced that theology needed to dialogue with the modern world. They believed that we needed a new language of faith in order to tell the Christian story in a faithful, credible, and intelligible manner. To meet the emerging crisis of faith, they looked to the past to inform the present—to the scriptures and the early church fathers.

For so long, theology has been a closed, static, and—at times—arrogant system. Its preoccupation with the need for certitude, with having answers for every question greatly impoverished the theological enterprise. Theology was losing its sense of the transcendent mystery who is the object of its study. Fortunately, there were those theologians among us who were attuned to the Spirit of God in the world. They found a way to break out of the fortress mentality of neoscholastic theology. The efforts of these new theologians produced a religious revitalization that was a far cry from the nonhistorical and rationalistic approach of neoscholasticism. They managed to do what great theologians must do: find a way to mediate the gospel to believers in their respective historical context. Saint Paul did it when he found a way to open the church to the gentiles in the first century. Thomas Aquinas did it when he managed to introduce Aristotle to Christianity. In this same tradition, Congar, Chenu, de Lubac, Rahner, and others found a way to tell the Christian story in a way that could transform the contemporary heart and soul.

These theologians shared something else as well. All of them found themselves officially disciplined in one way or another by church authorities in their day. But their stories did not end there. They would all come to be seen as the architects of the Second Vatican Council. In the chapters to follow, we discover the imprint of these great theologians in the documents of Vatican II, especially with regard to the church's attitude toward the world, toward the laity, toward itself.

2

THE CHURCH LOOKS
AT THE WORLD

Leading Up to Vatican II

The death of Pope Pius XII in 1958 marked the end of an era in the church's history. His papacy had provided the church with a strong, conservative leadership. At the conclave to elect his successor, we are told that the cardinals had difficulty coming to an agreement but, ultimately, reached a compromise. They elected seventy-seven-year-old Angelo Roncalli, who, they believed, would serve as an interim, transitional pope. No one at the time could have imagined what this new pope, John XXIII, would leave as his legacy.

Only three months after his election, John XXIII announced his decision to convene an ecumenical council. His announcement provoked a broad range of responses. But it is fair to say that, overall, the response of most people could be summed up in one word: Why? After all, Catholicism looked to be in pretty good shape at the time. Catholic schools were filled, vocations to the seminary and religious life were plentiful, and, thanks to their catechism, most Catholics "knew" the faith. So why a council? The question was important, too, because after the articulation of papal infallibility at the First Vatican Council (1869–70), no one thought there would ever be the need for another council. Pius XII had not only made one infallible pronouncement, the 1950 definition of the assumption into heaven of the Blessed Virgin Mary, but had also issued many (less authoritative) statements on many aspects of church life. What was John XXIII thinking? What prompted him to make such an incredible decision? As we would come to know, John credited the Holy Spirit as the inspiration for this announcement. It would appear that this great man took seriously the words of Jesus from John's Gospel: "The Advocate, the Holy Spirit…will teach you everything."[1]

Three years after this momentous announcement, the Second Vatican Council opened in October 1962. By the time it ended in 1965, it had produced sixteen documents—four constitutions, nine decrees, and three declarations—each of them addressing a central issue in the Catholic faith. This chapter looks at one of those issues: the relationship between the church and the world. The Pastoral Constitution on the Church in the Modern World, *Gaudium et Spes*, will serve as the context for this discussion.

To begin to grasp the significance of this document, we need to look at how the church viewed the world before the council. This view was the product of nearly two thousand years of history; a systematic treatment of those years would be beyond the scope of this book. Still, there are a number of aspects that most theologians would agree characterize the pre–Vatican II attitude toward the modern world. We examine a few of them here.

Dualism

This philosophy understood the world as the product of two forces—good and evil. Good was represented by spiritual reality and evil by material reality. In this system of thought, the world was seen as a place of exile and the human body as the prison of the soul. Though never officially espoused by the Catholic Church, dualism did leave its mark early on in Christian history. We see hints of it in the positions taken by such thinkers as Justin, Clement, Augustine, and Jerome—especially with regard to their teaching on sexual activity and marriage. We see it also in the distinction that came about between the celibate life and the married life, with celibacy being a higher state because of its purely spiritual status.[2]

Over the years, certain dualistic distinctions crept into our theological language as well. We would talk about the sacred versus the secular; the eternal versus the temporal; the supernatural versus the natural. Granted, there is a certain validity to these distinctions in some discussions, but using them as we did for so many years allowed a kind of dualism that clearly contributed to the church's disdain for the world. For one thing, we were far more concerned about the "next" world (heaven) than we were about "this" world (earth).

Defensive Stance

There is no doubt that in the one hundred years leading up to the Second Vatican Council, the prevailing attitude of the church toward the world could be referred to as a defensive mentality. We have the evidence of countless authors who use terms such as *fortress, defensive,* and *ghetto* to describe the church's mentality during those years.

The popes of the eighteenth and nineteenth centuries had been battling the forces of the modern world, particularly those of the Enlightenment, which led to the French Revolution of 1789, and secular movements toward democracy and freedom. Actually, the roots of this defensive, fortress mentality began even earlier, in reaction to the Protestant Reformation and the devastating collapse of Christian unity. For some reason, many in the church came to believe that the way to avoid such crises in the future would be to insulate the church behind a power structure that would claim to have all the answers. This unfortunate premise leads us to the next component, which played into the church's negative evaluation of the world in the years before Vatican II.

Classicist Thinking

For too long Catholic theology had been limited to the philosophy and theology of the Middle Ages. As we saw earlier, the popes of the eighteenth and nineteenth centuries jealously guarded the Scholastic approach to theology. But this classicist worldview is static and not open to the possibility of genuine development. One of Vatican II's best-known figures and a representative of the classicist mindset, Cardinal Ottaviani, chose as his episcopal motto, *Semper idem* ("Always the same"). Hence, truth is truth, the same today as yesterday—both in its content and in its articulation. This attitude can lead to a deadly arrogance and authoritarianism—a closed system that has little, if any, meaning for those who live outside the system. How then can the mission of the church to transform all things in Christ be accomplished if we refuse to speak to and listen to those outside the walls, walls that we ourselves erected?

Aggiornamento

Despite this long history of hostility to the modern world, John XXIII believed his council could be an *aggiornamento*, a bringing-up-to-date of the Catholic faith, adapting itself to meet the needs of modernity. And *Gaudium et Spes* was to be the centerpiece of this attempt. Even though this document came about after the death of John XXIII, it represents him more than any other council document. *Gaudium et Spes* expresses the most profound change from being a church in conflict with the world to being a church in dialogue with the world. It demonstrated a new consciousness in the church. It revealed a church in the direction of progress and serious renewal, a church no longer fearful of the world with which it shared a history. And, like John XXIII in his opening address at the council, *Gaudium et Spes* addressed itself not just to Catholics and other Christians, but to the whole of humanity, desiring to engage them and the world in authentic dialogue. As we shall see in our discussion of *Gaudium et Spes*, this dialogue would begin by focusing on the human person. If the church is to make a real contribution to the world, it will have to understand that world. The final draft of *Gaudium et Spes* passed with 1,710 votes in the affirmative; 480 of the council fathers voted against it. This last and longest of the council's documents was promulgated on December 7, 1965.

A few qualifying remarks are in order, however, before we take a closer look at *Gaudium et Spes*. It is appropriate to place them here because they impact not only our treatment of *Gaudium et Spes* in this chapter, but also all the Vatican II documents that are discussed in the course of this book.

Our discussion of each document does not propose to be an exhaustive one. Each of the sixteen documents contains rich theological insights and each could be the topic of a full-length book in itself. Rather, it is our purpose to look at the documents in light of how they evidence the remarkable change that was taking place in theology in the one hundred years between Vatican I and Vatican II. Hence, we have a very specific focus in mind.

The next point deals with what we might call the inherent problem in all the documents of Vatican II. This problem has been acknowledged by most council commentators and should be mentioned here for the sake of theological honesty. When one studies carefully the Second Vatican Council, it becomes very clear that—given the makeup of the participants—the sixteen documents they produced frequently bear the marks of compromise. Two distinct forces were at work at the council. They have been referred to as conservatives versus liberals, minority versus majority, dogmatic versus pastoral, and those holding on to established positions versus progressive thinkers. Such titles are rarely fair because they suggest an overly simplified designation. The truth is this: Regardless of which "camp" a particular council father represented, two things are clear about all of them: they loved their church and they tried to be attuned to the Holy Spirit in their midst.

Finally, a third point, of a personal nature. When I read these documents forty years after they were written, I wonder if the council fathers could have even imagined the far-reaching implications of the words they put on paper as the legacy of Vatican II. Many examples of this "wonderment" could be offered (and are, in the pages to follow) but one will suffice for now. In article 44 of *Gaudium et Spes*, we read:

> With the help of the Holy Spirit, it is the task of the entire People of God, especially pastors and theologians, to hear, distinguish and interpret the many voices of our age, and to judge them in the light of the divine word, so that revealed truth can always be more deeply penetrated, better understood and set forth to greater advantage.[3]

A remarkable paragraph, in that it contains so much—that the "whole" people of God are involved in this process, that we need to "hear" the many voices of our age, that truth can be "more deeply penetrated" and better understood. The council fathers could not possibly have foreseen the recent emergence of the Voice of the Faithful movement or questions about the role of women in the church, so controversial today. And yet, their words have provided a genuine opening for a discussion of such issues. Can anyone doubt the presence of the Holy Spirit in the council's deliberations?

A Document for Our Time

We are ready now to take a closer look at the central ideas of *Gaudium et Spes*. In the course of our discussion, it is hoped that we can show how *Gaudium et Spes* reflects the paradigm shifts discussed earlier as well as the deep relationship between these ideas and those prophetic theologians we met in chapter 1.

In that chapter, we looked at the three paradigm shifts that helped to change the way we did theology, a change that would ultimately lead us to Vatican II. Those shifts were from a classicist to a historically conscious worldview; from a deductive to an inductive methodology; from an apologetic to a foundational teaching style. We also looked at a group of prophetic theologians whose insights would result in a rethinking of such theological topics as incarnational theology, the historical method and the value of history as a theological category, the development of doctrine, pneumatology, Christology, a theological view of culture and theological anthropology. Our task now is to find evidence of this "new theology" in *Gaudium et Spes*.

Church and World: A Reconciliation

Gaudium et Spes is divided into two parts. Part I deals with the dignity of the human person, the human community, human activity, and the relationship between the church and the world. The second part addresses problems of special urgency: marriage and the family, human progress, life in its economic, social, and political dimensions, and the bonds between the family of nations.

The English title of this document, The Pastoral Constitution on the Church in the Modern World, reveals the first hint of a change regarding the church's attitude toward the world. It speaks of the church *in* the world—not *for* the world, or *toward* the world. *Gaudium et Spes* announces that the council focuses its attention on the world of men and women, the *whole* human family along with the sum of those realities in the midst of which it lives. It goes on to acknowledge the goodness of that world because it is created and sustained by God's love.[4] And, while acknowledging the basic goodness of the world, the document is also realistic about potential problems in the world, pointing to a "spirit of vanity and malice which transforms into an instrument of sin those human energies intended for the service of God and man."[5]

As we have seen, in the years leading up to the Second Vatican Council, efforts were being made by certain theologians to develop a more positive view of "the world." However, those attempts were rarely received with any enthusiasm by church officials. In fact, a number of official documents attest to this lack of enthusiasm. Perhaps the best known is *The Syllabus of Errors*, issued in 1864 by Pope Pius IX. In this document he condemned certain propositions that had been put forward by progressive thinkers at the time. Pius IX listed eighty errors of modern thinking, the last "error" causing great concern and confusion even at the time it was issued. In this one, the pope condemned the idea that the Roman Pontiff ought to reconcile himself with progress and with modern civilization.

In the years to follow, there were more official statements that revealed a certain mistrust, even condemnation, for the things of this world. Such disdain was usually directed at the "modern" world, an entity seen in opposition to the church. In 1879, Pope Leo XIII issued *Aeterni Patris* (On the Restoration of Christian Philosophy), in which he espoused Thomism as the cornerstone of Catholic orthodoxy. But it was a Thomism that was understood in an unhistorical way. This served to strengthen even more the narrow-thinking Scholastic movement, and Thomism became the only approach to be used in all theological schools at the time, thereby eliminating any new thinking from the modern world. However, a growing number of Catholic scholars did not agree that simply restoring a medieval approach to theology was the answer. They believed a broader dialogue between the church and the world was necessary if Catholicism was to remain a credible approach. These scholars were a rather loose coalition of thinkers, but all would ultimately be referred to as "Modernists." And, of course, they were not received well by the official church because they were daring to break through the wall of isolation that the church had erected to protect itself from the world, from modernity.

The Modernist debate continued for some time. In 1907, the decree known as *Lamentabili* was issued by the Holy Office in Rome, denouncing the Modernist ideas. Later that year, Pope Pius X followed up with an encyclical, *Pascendi*, in which he condemned what he referred to as "the heresies of Modernism." In fairness to the church officials at the time, some of the theological positions being advanced by some of the Modernists came close to being heretical and should have been condemned. The failure here was the refusal of the church to listen to the insights of the modern world, insights that were emerging from numerous academic disciplines such as archaeology, history, linguistics, psychology, and so on. Such a refusal resulted in the wall around Catholicism growing higher, and Catholicism and the world growing farther and farther apart.

Then, in 1950, another blow against the freedom for theological investigation, along with a rejection of insights from the world, came in the form of Pope Pius XII's encyclical *Humani Generis* (Of the Human Race). Though no individual theologian was named in this document, most agreed that this was Pius XII's attempt to quelle the "new theology." Like the popes before him, he cautioned Catholics about inherent problems in new and modern developments and claimed that Thomistic theology was to be the official theology of the church.

In an article written by Yves Congar, OP, twenty-five years after Vatican II, he discusses the church's understanding of the world both before and after Vatican II.[6] He says that Vatican II's view of what constituted the world of men and women, the temporal world, was incredibly comprehensive. He then compares Vatican II's attention to the "whole" with a work that was published in fifteen volumes between 1903 and 1950, *Dictionnaire de Theologie Catholique*. Amazingly, this dictionary of Catholic theology had no entries for the following topics: work, family, fatherhood, motherhood, friendship, sex, pleasure, joy, suffering, economy, politics, technology, beauty, value, or world. However, the word *evil* had twenty-five columns of treatment and "the power of the pope in the temporal world" received 103 columns of discussion. By way of contrast, *Gaudium et Spes* becomes even more remarkable and revelatory of the change that was taking place in the church's theology of the world.

As time passes, however, it becomes harder and harder to make this point, because the pre–Vatican II Catholic way of life and thinking in many ways no longer exists, except perhaps in the minds of those who are old enough to have lived in "both churches." But even some of them have forgotten the way things were. And, for post–Vatican II generations, this former view is simply unknown. On December 17, 1965—just days after Vatican II ended—*Time* magazine printed an insightful article entitled, "How Vatican II Turned the Church toward the World."[7] In its treatment of the church-world relationship before and after Vatican II, it quoted two men very close to the council's activities. It is worth noting their comments here for those who may have forgotten the impact of *Gaudium et Spes* and for those who never knew the significance of this moment. With regard to the church before Vatican II, the English Benedictine Abbot, Dom Christopher Butler, claimed, "Before, the church looked like an immense, immovable colossus, the city set on a hill, the stable bulwark against the revolutionary change."[8] Then, commenting on the enormous change brought about by Vatican II, specifically in *Gaudium et Spes*, India's Archbishop Eugene D'Souza remarked, "The church's whole approach to the world is one of sincere admiration, not of dominating it, but of serving it, not of despising it but of appreciating it, not of condemning it but of strengthening it and saving it."[9] So, despite a history of mistrust, disdain, often outright condemnation, the church had reconciled with the world. Such a moment was the result of many factors, some of which must be now examined more closely.

A Changing Theology

At the very beginning of *Gaudium et Spes*, we discover a new methodology at work. Article 2 states, "Therefore, the Council focuses its attention on the world of men, the whole human family along with the sum of those realities in the midst of which it lives; that world which is the theatre of man's history...."[10] In the very next article, we read, "Hence, the focal point of our total presenta-

45

tion will be man himself, whole and entire, body and soul, heart and conscience, mind and will."[11] Here, unlike previous official church documents, whose starting points would be the truths of the faith, *Gaudium et Spes* suggests a very different starting point: the human person. This document demonstrates a clear shift from a deductive methodology to an inductive methodology, a shift that will open the door to an entirely changed treatment of the church-world relationship. Because *Gaudium et Spes* begins its examination with the human condition, with experiences that are common to believers and nonbelievers alike, a new light will be cast on issues such as the possibility of salvation for all, the inherent goodness of the created world, the plurality of cultures, and the ultimate vocation and destiny of the human person. Christianity has always claimed that its message was a universal message, but that claim becomes all the more credible now because, by beginning with the reality of human existence and the world with which it shares a history, the message of *Gaudium et Spes* becomes accessible to all humans, not just those within the Catholic family.

As we saw in the previous chapter, this shift from a deductive to an inductive methodology did not begin at the Second Vatican Council. The seeds were being sown long before John XXIII's inspiration to convene a council. The writings of so many theologians were paving the way for Vatican II.

Romano Guardini was one of the earliest proponents of the kind of thinking that would emerge at the council. Like *Gaudium et Spes*, Guardini's theology began with the basic concerns and questions his listeners had in their concrete situations, not with issues and topics within theology itself, not with a system of timeless truths, though quite valid in and of themselves.[12] Theology must always find a language of life, one that men and women of any given generation can understand.

Guardini was, of course, in good company in his use of the inductive method. Yves Congar was also a forerunner in this methodology. Commenting years later on *Gaudium et Spes*'s attempt to speak of the church in the world, Congar claimed "an investigative, descriptive, and inductive method was indicated....The church must ask questions of the world; she must listen to the 'others.'"[13] Congar spoke quite emphatically to the need for this new methodology, claiming that if theology remains at the level of intellectual activity alone, remote from the real world, it is a dead theology because theology must listen to and try to respond to the questions men and women have. It cannot be merely deductive.[14]

Inductive methodology was also at the heart of M.-D. Chenu's theology. His understanding of the church-world relationship was led by the model of incarnation. For Chenu, the incarnation did not merely occur once and for all two thousand years ago when the divine entered the human condition in a unique manner in the person of Jesus of Nazareth. Rather, incarnation continues through history in every human person. He maintained that the church in every historical period is being called to new ways of being present to the world, that each and every change requires a new incarnation.[15]

The idea of incarnational theology, so central to Chenu's theology, is but a manifestation of the inductive method. The examination of the human condition yields a "being" whose desires cannot be completely fulfilled by this world alone. As discussed previously, anthropology by its very nature posits a theology, since questions about the human person lead to questions about God. Theologians came to see the validity of the inductive approach because the human condition in and of itself can be a source of truth in the theological enterprise. As we shall see, the implications are far-reaching. Chenu agrees "that a study of anthropology would figure prominently in any theology and that it would include a position on the concrete human situation."[16] In the same way, *Gaudium et Spes* sees the world of men and women, human progress and the development of this concrete world as a good thing, and cautions us that "the expectation of a new earth must not weaken...our concern for cultivating this one...for here grows the body of a new human family...able to give some kind of foreshadowing of the new age."[17] One can almost envision Chenu writing these words because he too believed that the care and cultivation of this world is all part of an ongoing incarnation leading to a final transformation. He knew that to view the church as a continuous incarnation meant we would have to overcome the dualism between church and world. This means taking the concrete historical situation of men and women seriously. As John XXIII invited us to read "the signs of the times,"[18] Chenu did as well. He saw these "signs" as opportunities for the gospel to take root in any given human situation. The incarnation occurs in creation itself. Hence, the church is not outside of the world. Because of this, "human events, values, and the project of constructing the world, all are of interest to the church."[19]

Theological Anthropology

By choosing the human person as the starting point for its church-world relationship, *Gaudium et Spes* made clear the necessity of a sound theological anthropology. The council fathers would have to address this question: What does it mean to be human?

The understanding of humanity as outlined in the introduction and first four chapters of *Gaudium et Spes* is the most exhaustive and theologically rich treatment that can be found in the council documents. As we examine some of these insights we will see the imprint of those theologians who clearly prepared the soil for such an inspired theology.

A key issue in theological anthropology is the attempt to understand the divine-human relationship. We saw earlier that, from the Middle Ages on, there had been a tendency to make a sharp distinction between the supernatural and the natural, between grace and nature, as though they were two completely separate entities. In this line of thinking, grace becomes something "added on" to human nature. Such an approach opens the door for a dualistic understanding of humanity. All things spiritual, for example, grace, are good, and all material realities, for example, human nature, are…well, if not evil, then certainly less good. This separation between grace and nature had serious repercussions for believers in the decades before Vatican II. We could simply never be good enough, we could never "be perfect as our heavenly Father was perfect."[20] This great gap between God and us (as we perceived it) led to a great deal of guilt and frustration. And, when you view grace as a "thing" you can get, it also becomes a "thing" you can lose. Hence, we came to believe that we could "lose" God as a result of a serious sin.

This dualistic approach to the divine-human relationship flourished in the years between Vatican I and Vatican II. However, something else was occurring in some theological circles. A new understanding of the grace-nature relationship was being suggested by "the new theologians," men like Henri de Lubac and Karl Rahner. As noted in chapter 1, de Lubac was convinced that nature was made for the supernatural. And, according to Rahner, "Man's experience of himself is always an experience of God."[21] And, as we saw in a previous discussion of Rahner, rather than speak about grace as something "added on" to nature, Rahner preferred to speak about our "graced nature."

In the same vein, John Henry Newman was preaching that humans had a capacity for a relationship between our soul and the God who made it.[22] And, as to the decisive element that constitutes the human condition, as early as 1921, Romano Guardini responded that it is to be "called forth by God."[23]

The essence of what these theologians were claiming can be stated as follows: "God does not come as a stranger to any human soul. The grace of Christ...comes to dwell in a home prepared for its reception....He endowed every man with something more than a primeval indifference to the divine touch."[24] Or as Rahner so succinctly wrote, "God is not a foreign term for man."[25] We are reminded of the well-known quote of Saint Augustine: "God is more intimate to me than I am to myself."

This theological anthropology is grounded in a solid theological principle: humanity was created by God, for God. We were created in such a way that it is in our very nature to have a capacity to receive the supernatural. At the creative moment, God is not merely giving us truths about himself—we are given a presence. "The giver is the gift himself."[26]

Years later, at Vatican II, this very approach to the divine-human relationship would find expression in the council documents, specifically in *Gaudium et Spes*. Sounding very similar to Guardini, article 19 states, "The root reason for human dignity lies in man's call to communion with God. From the very circumstance of his origin man is already invited to converse with God."[27] More evidence of this thinking is found in article 14. It speaks about humanity's interior qualities, claiming that the human person "plunges into the depths of reality whenever he enters his own heart; God, who probes the heart, awaits him there."[28]

It is commonplace in theological circles today to speak like this about grace. Theologians speak about "mediated immediacy." In the realm of my very being, I do have an "immediate" experience of God since God is present at the core of my being. But in the realm of my consciously knowing about this experience, it is a "mediated" experience.[29] But such thinking was not so common in the decades before Vatican II. Clearly, the theologians we have looked at were breaking new ground, suffering because of it, and ultimately being vindicated when the fathers at Vatican II adopted this theologically rich anthropology.

Christ the Key Element in a Theological Anthropology

Gaudium et Spes gives evidence of another aspect of the theological anthropology proposed by many of the new theologians—that Jesus Christ is the ultimate key to understanding the human condition. Article 38 offers an excellent summary of this point:

> It has been entrusted to the church to reveal the mystery of God....She opens up to man the innermost truths about himself. The church knows that only God...meets the deepest longings of the human heart, which is never fully satisfied by what this world has to offer....Only God, who created man to his own image...provides the most adequate answers to the questions (of man), and this [the church] does...through Christ...who became man.[30]

In a similar passage dealing with the ultimate anthropological question—What is man?—article 10 responds, "(The church) holds that in her most benign Lord and Master can be found the key, the focal point and the goal of man, as well as of all human history...under the light of Christ...the Council wishes...to shed light on the mystery of man."[31]

In this regard, Karl Rahner refers to Jesus Christ as "the absolute bringer of salvation."[32] Rahner's basis for this claim is this: Through the life, death, and resurrection of Jesus Christ, the possibility of salvation for all humans becomes a reality. Article 22 of *Gaudium et Spes* supports this claim: "By his incarnation the Son of God has united himself with every man."[33]

A good number of the new theologians developed a solid christological approach in their theological reflections. As early as 1929, Romano Guardini spoke about Jesus Christ himself as the essence of Christianity. Guardini acknowledged the significance of church teachings and the Christian meaning of life, but, he insisted, at the very center of Christianity is Jesus Christ—his existence, his work, his destiny.[34] Guardini's christological focus becomes even more significant, because at a time when theology focused so heavily on the divine nature of Jesus Christ, Guardini was working diligently to recover the humanity of Christ. If, as *Gaudium et Spes* claims, Jesus Christ is truly the answer to humanity's questions, then the reality of his human nature becomes a critical issue for believers.

Inculturation

The implications of the inductive approach in *Gaudium et Spes* are many. In making the human person the focal point of their deliberations, the council fathers also opened the door for a renewed consideration of human culture. This was a direct result of the inductive method that belongs to incarnational theology. Just as the Word of God assumed the human condition in a particular place and at a particular time, so too the church must become incarnate in various places, times, and people. The very word catholic requires this. Catholicism claims to have a universal message for all of humanity. Hence, it must be possible for the Christian story to take root and flourish in any and all cultures, and it must be done in a way that respects the individual elements of a given culture.

However, the history of the church, especially from the Middle Ages on, has not always demonstrated a healthy relationship with human culture. The attempts to truly evangelize other cultures have not been as successful as they might have been. The fault lies not with the individual cultures, but with the church's method. As the church moved through history, an overly central-ized view of church structure developed, with the church of Rome at its center. The whole church came to be identified with the church of Rome. One might compare it to a corporate model. The "main office" was in Rome, with the various local churches all over the world viewed as "branch offices," or franchises. The language, liturgy, and customs of Rome were considered normative for all churches. It was as though the church of Rome had been cloned, many times over. (We should note here the importance of the Eastern Churches that remained in communion with Rome. They were very precious in maintaining traditions different from the Western Latin Church.) But the corporate model of the Western Church would of course affect the church's missionary activities. It meant that potential converts came to feel that to accept Christianity would involve giving up their own culture and adopting the Western, Eurocentric vision imposed on them by Rome.

Gaudium et Spes represents a major break away from this model of evangelization. It recognized humanity's sacred connec-tion to individual cultures. In article 44, we read, "The experience of past ages…and the treasures hidden in the various forms of human culture, by…which the nature of man himself is more clearly revealed and new roads to truth are opened, these profit the church."[35] This article goes on to speak about the need to adapt the gospel to the needs of all and then boldly states, "Indeed, this accommodated preaching of the revealed word ought to remain the law of evangelization…(calling for) a living exchange between the church and the diverse cultures of people."[36] For anyone familiar with the mostly pre–Vatican II missionary approaches, this was indeed an amazing claim. An equally striking acceptance of culture comes later in the document: "Man comes to a true and full humanity only through culture.…Wherever human life is involved, therefore…nature and culture are quite intimately connected one with the other."[37] Yesterday's missionaries, men like Matteo Ricci, Robert de Nobili, and others, who had supported this understand-ing of missionary activity long before the official church subscribed to it, would have been very pleased with Vatican II's understanding of culture, especially its recognition of "a plurality of cultures."[38] This is inductive theology at its best. How else can the church bring the good news to the world of men and women if it refuses to take seriously and respectfully the realities of that world? Even so, the council fathers were careful to present a balanced view of the value of culture. The ultimate norm is always the gospel itself, prompting them to remind us that "the church...is not bound exclusively and indissolubly to any race or nation, any particular way of life or any customary way of life recent or ancient."[39]

Reasons to Believe

We have seen how the council fathers embraced the paradigm shift from a deductive to an inductive methodology. We move now to a brief discussion of the shift that changed the way we did theology, from an apologetic to a foundational style of teaching.

Catholic believers were indeed growing up. The argument from authority was no longer an adequate way to teach the faith. Catholics needed reasons to believe. They had to move beyond the memorized answers of the catechism and come to terms with what they believed and why they believed it. The council fathers agreed: "We can justly consider that the future of humanity lies in the hands of those who are strong enough to provide coming generations with reasons for living and hoping."[40]

For decades before Vatican II, theologians were advancing this very claim. They were moving away from an emphasis on simply proclaiming a truth of the faith to an emphasis on understanding that truth. Granted, there are certain truths of Christianity that are beyond the finite human's ability to fully comprehend, for example, the Trinity and the resurrection. But the point these theologians wanted to make is this: The Christian story is reasonable. It makes sense. It speaks to the deepest needs of the human condition. And, in the footsteps of Saint Anselm's famous statement, *Fides quaerens intellectum* ("Faith seeks understanding"), these prophets among us were doing just that—making the act of faith reasonable. They were giving reasons to believe. Humans will not commit themselves heart and soul, mind and body to what they do not know. This was becoming increasingly clear in the decades prior to Vatican II. Something remarkable was occurring in the field of theology. Change was taking place not only in the way we did theology but also in how the very task of the theologian was understood.

In the years between Vatican I and Vatican II, the source for theology was the official teaching office of the church, the Magisterium. It was a theology that was based on papal encyclicals and magisterial utterances. In a sense, Catholic theology became locked in a "non-historical system of timeless truths."[41] As we saw in an earlier discussion, in such a situation the task of a theologian looks more like being a mere mouthpiece for official teaching. He or she simply articulates magisterial teachings for others. But more and more theologians were becoming dissatisfied with this perception. Like John Henry Newman, they were becoming convinced that Catholicism must be defended "by reason, not by force."[42] Like Yves Congar, they came to understand that "it is not authority which makes the truth, it is truth which judges authority."[43] Like the Tübingen theologian, Johann Sebastian von Drey, they came to see a new role for the theologian, because the characteristic thrust of Christian doctrine is that it must unfold. Hence, "the goal of theology is not only the maintenance but its furtherance."[44] And, like Karl Rahner, they agreed on the absolute need "to make theology respectable in the modern world…to place theology at the service of Christian faith and life."[45] Rahner was convinced that the traditional teaching about the faith must be tested against humanity's experience of itself in the modern world. These theologians believed that they needed to demonstrate how the Christian faith answered the desires and questions of men and women in the world.

It would seem their voices were heard. In his opening address at the Second Vatican Council, Pope John XXIII clearly embraced the foundational style of teaching. He announced, "The church prefers to make use of the medicine of mercy rather than that of severity…demonstrating the validity of her teachings rather than by condemnations."[46] *Gaudium et Spes* supported this claim: "For the Council yearns to explain to everyone how it conceives of the presence and activity of the church in the world of today."[47] It yearns to *explain*. This was quite simply a remarkable development.

Indeed, theology had changed. The task of a theologian had changed as well. In a discussion regarding the freedom of contemporary theologians, Cardinal Walter Kasper remarked, "Today...theology must dare to ask deeper and more biting questions....It must become in truth, *'fides quaerens intellectum.'*"[48]

A Renewed Sense of History

We now turn to a discussion of the third paradigm shift that had a hand in changing theology in the years leading up to the Second Vatican Council. It was a shift in worldview from a classicist to an historically conscious perspective. The prevailing worldview prior to the council was clearly classicist. It saw truth as static, unchanging, and, in fact, unaffected by history. Truth is contained in propositions that are fixed and certain and can be articulated in more or less the same way from one generation to another. Historical consciousness takes a very different approach to the transmission of truths. It appreciates the role of history. It recognizes that all expressions of theological truth are historically conditioned, products of a concrete moment in history and therefore affected by that moment. An authentically historically conscious approach does not deteriorate into relativism, a position that fails to yield absolutes. The truths of revelation do not change, but the way that humans understand and express these truths reflect the given time period. They undergo growth and development. Just as humankind's own self-understanding grows and develops, so too does humanity's grasp of revelation. This is not to say there is no value attached to the classicist approach. Its strengths would be a desire for clarity, an articulation that is precise, and a level of objectivity. The historically conscious view must take care to incorporate these very positive components.

How did the church move from the classicist to the historically conscious mindset, which, as we shall see, finds a home in the theology of Vatican II? The answer to this question can be found in the many remarkable theological insights offered by those new theologians at work in the years before the council. They were convinced that a return to the sources as a foundation for doing theology would yield a rich harvest.

A renewed appreciation of history was a critical component for these theologians. The Tübingen School of Theology in Germany was one of the great centers for this renewal. Its members believed that history was the arena where the growth and manifestation of the plan of salvation occurs, because we are moving toward the realization of God's kingdom. This emphasis on the value of history was certainly a key element in that *nouvelle theologie* in the years before Vatican II.

It was clearly at the heart of John Henry Newman's theology. He knew that if the faith was to retain its vitality, if it was to meet the needs of a given people at a given time and a given place, then the living church "will sometimes have to articulate its faith in new ways."[49] In fact, one of Newman's best-known works is his *Essay on the Development of Doctrine*.[50] In this work, Newman sought to explain that new insights in our grasp of the faith are not necessarily distortions, but can be legitimate developments. Sometimes the example of an "onion" is used to talk about this concept (sometimes, simple is best). We could imagine the basic truths of revelation at the center of the onion, and the task of each generation—with their unique questions and concerns—is to peel away a layer of the onion, permitting more light, if you will, to illuminate the richness of the center. It should be noted that Newman also provided numerous "tests" to be used in the discernment process, determining the legitimacy of any given development. Important to note as well that by the end of the nineteenth century, this idea of the development of doctrine was widely accepted in the Catholic Church.

This idea of viewing the faith as a living, developing organism affected by history was taken up by many of the new theologians in the years leading up to the council. For Chenu, the incarnation did not simply occur once and for all two thousand years ago, but continues through history. He maintained that the church in every historical period is being called to new ways of being present to the world, that each and every change requires a new incarnation. This, perhaps, explains one of Chenu's favorite themes: "God speaks today."[51] Our concrete, historical circumstances must be taken seriously because in them the Word of God is present.

This same appreciation for the ongoing development and understanding of doctrine was also advanced by Congar. For him, the plan of salvation is not a fixed, static reality. Rather "it is a history and a development inserted into time and disclosing little by little its meaning and value."[52] He used the metaphor of a seed that already contains a fullness, but only arrives at its completion after the stages of development.[53]

This understanding of growth and development of theological truth is actually grounded in a deeper truth: the Christian God is best described as mystery. Rahner best expressed the relationship between the two: "Mystery is not that which I cannot know. Mystery is that which I cannot exhaust."[54]

Perhaps the first glimpse that Vatican II would embrace this historically conscious worldview came in the opening address of John XXIII at the council, where he made the distinction between the ancient deposit of the faith and the way it is expressed for every generation.[55] In many ways, this opening address set the tone for the documents that would ultimately emerge at the conclusion of Vatican II. This is certainly true for *Gaudium et Spes*, which quoted the distinction made by the pope in that opening statement.[56] Also included in this particular passage from *Gaudium et Spes* was a statement that must have brought great joy to those theologians whose prophetic insights had been dismissed by some leaders of the official church over the years. The council fathers acknowledged the need to take seriously the questions posed by modernity, claiming:

> The recent studies and findings of science, history and philosophy raise new questions which affect life and which demand new theological investigations. Furthermore, theologians, within the requirements and methods proper to theology, are invited to seek continually for more suitable ways of communicating doctrine to the men of their times.[57]

Another acknowledgment of the historically conscious worldview occurs earlier in *Gaudium et Spes*: "The human race has passed from a rather static concept of reality to a more dynamic, evolutionary one."[58]

Theology is never about making isolated statements of fact. Every theological expression is rich with potential implications and *Gaudium et Spes*'s acceptance of a new worldview is a good example of this point. Toward the end of the document, the council fathers made a very significant comment: "While (this Council) presents teaching already accepted in the church, the program will have to be followed up and amplified since it sometimes deals with matters in a state of development."[59] The importance of this statement was not lost on commentators. Church historian John O'Malley, SJ, noted that for the first time, this church gathering appeared to be aware of its own mortality, that they were not uttering the final word.[60] Yves Congar, OP, also weighed in on this momentous moment in church history. If, as *Gaudium et Spes* states, the ideas set forth by Vatican II will need to be followed up and amplified, then, according to Congar, "Reform here will be the willingness to adapt the structure of ecclesial life to a new situation."[61]

This willingness to adapt was at the very heart of the church in its earliest days. The New Testament witnesses to this fact. Though united in the essential truths of the faith, the earliest Christian communities were distinguished by their "situation." The local church of Rome, for example, was different from other local churches such as Ephesus, Corinth, Jerusalem, and so on. As new concerns and questions emerged, the local churches developed structures to meet those needs. This awareness was one of the greatest benefits resulting from the new theologians' "return to the sources" as the foundation for doing theology.

Conclusion

The history of the church's understanding of the world, of modernity, is a complex one. But it is fair to say that in the decades prior to the Second Vatican Council, the church's view of the world was not a positive one. We have tried to show in this chapter how Vatican II reflected a number of changes that had taken place in theology, changes that would enhance the way we looked at the modern world.

These changes were due to certain paradigm shifts that were emerging over the years. We have discussed those shifts and demonstrated how a number of remarkable theologians, so attuned to the presence of the Holy Spirit in their theological endeavors, brought about a very significant change in the way we came to understand the modern world, a world with which it shared a history. We came to see the world as a genuine partner in dialogue. The fidelity of these prophetic voices triumphed over the many obstacles placed in their paths. Their search for truth and their desire to articulate that truth brought us to an incredible moment in church history. And, perhaps, we will never know the full price that has been paid by these great theologians for Vatican II.[62] Still, to be a prophet is to speak on behalf of God, and that is never an easy task.

Gaudium et Spes, the Pastoral Constitution on the Church in the Modern World, is by far one of the most important documents of the Second Vatican Council. In their use of the word *pastoral*, the council fathers wanted to present the truths of the faith in a manner that would speak to contemporary men and women, take seriously their difficulties, and try to answer their questions. Accepting the inherent goodness of the world, created and sustained by God, *Gaudium et Spes* offered us a new way of looking at the world, of caring for the world, of serving the world. Earlier, we made reference to an essay that appeared at the end of Vatican II, referring to the church-world relationship. Its concluding lines bear repeating:

> When medieval Popes spoke to Kings and Princes, they listened and obeyed, or ran the risk of excommunication. The words of Pope Paul VI and his bishops to Presidents and Premiers bear no such threat; but neither did those of the Apostles to the Roman procurators. Thus the more the church returns in spirit to the unfettered simplicity of the Gospel from which it sprang, the more likely it is that its voice will be heeded again by the world.[63]

3

THE CHURCH LOOKS
AT THE LAITY

The Layperson in the Church before Vatican II

It might strike contemporary readers as odd that an entire chapter would be devoted to the relationship between the church and the laity. After all, for the past forty years we have been referring to the church as "the people of God." Clearly, since Vatican II, the laity has enjoyed a position of importance in the life of the church. With the decline in vocations to the priesthood and religious life—previously the primary evangelizers in the church—the laity have now embraced a variety of ministries.

However, this has not always been the case. In this book, we have been examining the years before Vatican II, discussing the theological developments that paved the way for the Second Vatican Council. And, in this chapter, we take a brief look at the history of the laity's place in the church and how they were viewed in the years leading up to the council. We also look at the efforts of the "new theologians" to improve the laity's role and offer some theological principles that serve as a foundation for an authentic theology of the laity and, finally, demonstrate how these theological efforts and principles ultimately found a home in the Vatican II documents—in particular *Lumen Gentium* (the Dogmatic Constitution on the Church), *Gaudium et Spes* (the Pastoral Constitution on the Church in the Modern World), and *Apostolicam Actuositatem* (Decree on the Apostolate of the Laity).

Struggling to Find a Voice

When asked about the role of the laity in the mid-nineteenth century, Monsignor George Talbot, an English curial official who had served as secretary to Pope Pius IX, responded, "To hunt, to shoot, to entertain. These matters they understand, but to meddle with ecclesiastical matters, they have no right at all."[1] This quote is a good indication of how the laity was viewed in the church in the years leading up to Vatican II. There was a marked division between the clergy and the laity, between the sacred and the secular, between the eternal and the temporal. We can trace the beginnings of this division as far back as the fourth century, but it would be given a significant place by the time of the Middle Ages when theologians divided the church into separate states: the *ordo clericorum* (clergy) and the *ordo laicorum* (laity).[2]

This separation of clergy from laity was further enhanced by a model of church that emerged during the second millennium, one that would ultimately prevail right up to the eve of the Second Vatican Council. We say more about this model in the next chapter but, given its impact on the role of the laity, it needs to be addressed in this context.

Anyone trained in Catholicism before Vatican II would be familiar with this model, frequently referred to as the "pyramid" model of church. This pyramid reflected one's place in the church. At the top was the pope, followed by cardinals, bishops, priests, nuns, and—last—the laity. It was a "rank-and-file" approach. The higher one's place on the pyramid, the holier one was (or so we thought.) In this model, those at the top "had" the truth, those below "received" the truth. (In fairness, it should be noted that until just before Vatican II, serious theological education was reserved for members of the clergy.)

As a result of this division between cleric and layperson, it was understood that the mission of the church was in the hands of the hierarchy. It was "their" apostolate, and any involvement of the laity in this work was understood as "assisting" the hierarchy with their ministry. That the layperson had the right, even the duty, for an apostolate of their own in the church's mission was simply not considered.

The Road to Vatican II

Yves Congar was one of the first of the new theologians to begin working out a theology of the laity, obviously a very controversial move during his day, considering the prevailing model of church. Referring to those who might see such an attempt as "dangerous," Congar quotes a reply of the bishop of Dijon, Monsignor Dadolle, to a similar objection in 1907. This quote is presented in full since it reflects the problem so convincingly:

> It is very possible that in the past we bishops did not understand your role sufficiently and completely enough. We used to appeal to your purse for our material needs, to your devotedness...to your devotion for the carrying of a candle in a procession. If that was nearly all, it was not, or at any rate is not, enough....Over centuries, apostleship was looked upon as a "reversed occupation," and at least in practice the distinction between teachers and taught, priests and lay folk, increased to excess....There is the discussion of the delicate question of coordinating the two apostleships...hierarchical and lay....I am well aware of the dangers that there are. The only way to avoid them is to do nothing....But that is to resign ourselves to the worst evil of all, standing aloof: the part chosen by those useless souls to whom Dante in his Hell would vouchsafe no gleam of pity, but...look and pass by.[3]

Here we have an excellent insight into the laity's role in the preconciliar church, a church that was primarily hierarchical, a church centered on the role of the cleric, a church that clearly marginalized the function of the layperson in ecclesial matters.

Fortunately, at the same time there were those theologians whose insights and efforts were about to change this image, resulting in a significant—and long overdue—development in the vocation of the layperson in the church.

Return to the Sources

The church is divinely founded and divinely guided, but it has been in the hands of humans for more than two thousand years. As an organization of humans it runs the same risk of all organizations: the farther away it gets from the moment of its original founding and from the charism of the original founder, it sometimes loses touch with that charism...hence, the constant need to reform, renew, restore.

In the years before Vatican II, the new theologians saw the need to return to the original sources of the Christian Church. In doing that, they came to distinguish some distortions that had crept into the life of the church. One such distortion was the sharp division between the clergy and the laity. Their study of the New Testament yielded many theological insights. One would have a direct bearing on the development of a theology of the laity.

In the Acts of the Apostles, chapter 15, we read about the Council of Jerusalem, the very first council in the church's history. It was called to settle a serious dispute in the early days of the church. The issue was basically this: how to reconcile the admission of gentiles into the church, given the fact that these gentiles did not live according to the Mosaic Law and its practices. As we read in chapter 15, agreement was reached in this matter not only by the apostles and the presbyters, but "with the consent of the whole church."[4] During their discussion, Peter stood up and offered a theological foundation for the inclusion of these gentiles: "And God, who knows the human heart, testified to them by giving them the Holy Spirit, just as he did to us."[5] This "giving of the Holy Spirit" to all believers would become the cornerstone of a theology of the laity. As our new theologians continued to study the New Testament, they read in the Letter to the Ephesians, "There is one body and one Spirit, just as you were called to the one hope of your calling, one Lord, one faith, one baptism, one God and Father of all, who is above all and through all and in all."[6] The Letter to the Ephesians goes on to speak about a diversity of gifts—that some would be apostles, some prophets, some pastors, some teachers...that the whole body would grow, with the proper functioning of each gift.

Through their reading of the New Testament, theologians came to realize that for years the church had neglected an essential component of its original foundation: the "pneumatological" component, the role of the Holy Spirit. The ecclesiology of the pre–Vatican II church had emphasized the christological component, the role of Jesus Christ in the founding of the church, but it seemed to forget the Holy Spirit. With this "rediscovery" of the Holy Spirit's role, coupled with the theological implications of the granting of the Spirit to every believer at baptism, the road to uncovering the very essential place for the laity in the church was underway.

The New Testament speaks of the many gifts that go into the building up of the body of Christ. This same principle could be applied to the many theologians who would ultimately "build" a theology of the laity in the church. Each brought his own charism as well as his own theological concern to the study of the layperson. And, from a theological point of view, these many voices were an indispensable part of the process because a sound theology of the laity would require a foundation rooted in solid theological principles.

A Theology of Communion

Yves Congar attended the Second Vatican Council and served as a *peritus*, a theological expert. At one point during the council, Congar was thinking about his own theological past and wrote:

> Perhaps the church will be surprised to find herself so firmly convinced of things she scarcely realized only a few years ago. Who sowed this seed? And who sowed it in me some thirty-five years ago? One might as well ask who makes the dawn succeed night, or spring follow winter?[7]

Like so many of his colleagues in theology, Congar was convinced that the council could truly be a moment of grace for the church. He had worked for decades in anticipation of such a moment and he left his mark on so many of the council's teachings. Vatican II's treatment of the laity would, without doubt, be one of these teachings.

We saw earlier that the pyramid model of church prevailed in the years leading up to Vatican II. Perhaps the most serious problem with this model is that it finds no home in the New Testament. What Congar and many of his colleagues *did* find in their study of the New Testament was a *communio* model of church, rooted in the presence of the Holy Spirit in each member of the community. It is a model that is in sharp contrast to the pyramid model. In the next chapter, we look at the church itself, and the contrast between the two models is more fully developed. For now, a brief discussion of the *communio* model and its relationship to the role of the laity will suffice.

The word *communio* means "fellowship, responsible fellowship," and this is the hallmark of New Testament ecclesiology. As early as 1937, Congar was rediscovering this model of church and was writing about the role of the Holy Spirit in a theology of communion. The significance of this theological principle cannot be overstated, as the implications are so central to the New Testament understanding of church. If, as Congar believes, the Holy Spirit is the "soul" of the church,[8] given to each member at baptism, then the notion of the church as the "people of God," building up the body of Christ with the individual gifts and charisms of the faithful, means that each member has a truly significant role to play in the mission of the church. Each person, cleric or lay, has a legitimate voice. Each member can be a source of truth.

As mentioned, this theology of communion is revisited in the next chapter on the church's self-understanding. There we will see how it opens the door for an authentic approach to collegiality in the church, to the concept of reception of church teaching by the faithful, to a move beyond a juridical, monarchical model of church to the notion of the church as the "people of God" on their way to the fullness of truth, who is God.

However, since a theology of communion, grounded in the presence of the Spirit in all baptized members, is truly a foundational principle for a theology of the laity, we include it in this chapter as well.

The *Sensus Fidelium*

One very important component of a theology of communion is a concept known as the *sensus fidelium*, the "sense of the faithful." It holds that the Holy Spirit is active in the whole church. The term indicates that the church's teaching emerges out of the faith of the entire church and is evidence of a mutuality between hierarchical authority and the faithful in the formulation of doctrine.

Sensus fidelium is a concept that has a long history in the tradition of the church. However, due to—among other things—the emergence of the pyramid model of the church during the second millennium, it had been neglected and generally forgotten. As one of our "new theologians," M.-D. Chenu, pointed out, "Only in the twentieth century…did the church rediscover its heritage in this area."[9]

Still, there had been efforts to rediscover this sense of the faithful even before the twentieth century. In 1859, John Henry Newman published his work *On Consulting the Faithful in Matters of Doctrine*.[10] According to Newman, the body of the faithful, by virtue of their baptism, have an infused sense of the faith, a kind of instinct, by which they accept authentic teaching and reject false teaching.[11] This view was not received well at all by the hierarchy at the time. Some of them were infuriated by Newman's claim that the laity should be consulted in matters of doctrine. Newman's vindication on this point would finally come one hundred years later at Vatican II in *Lumen Gentium*, which spoke of a supernatural sense of the faith possessed by the whole people of God.[12]

This understanding of the role of the Holy Spirit functioning in the faithful is echoed again and again by the new theologians in the years before the council (and afterward as well). As early as 1936, Karl Rahner was suggesting that baptism provided each member of the church with a mission of pastoral care.[13] According to Rahner, the basis for this is quite simple: "The source of unity between…the charisms of the hierarchy and the laity was itself the origin of those charisms: the Holy Spirit."[14]

These theologians were clearly preparing the way for the documents of Vatican II and for the role that would be given to the Holy Spirit in those documents (for example, the Holy Spirit receives 252 references). The council fathers realized that the church was a community in which the gifts of the Holy Spirit are available to all the members. Vatican II would rediscover the critical relationship between pneumatology and ecclesiology.

It was noted previously that one reason the concept of *sensus fidelium* appeared to fall by the wayside in church teaching was the pyramid model of church that had prevailed in the years before the council. And, it is a basic theological principle that one's definition of church will also yield a definition of the laity's role in the church. Earlier in the chapter we examined, though briefly, the pyramid model of church. This ecclesiology is not conducive to dialogue in the church, nor is it open to input from the members. Hence, it is easy to see how the concept of *sensus fidelium* came to be neglected, even ignored, over the years. This neglect opened the door to additional problems. For the *sensus fidelium* to function effectively, the members have to receive a sound religious education. They need to be taught and encouraged to think critically, to allow reason to inform faith. They need to know the existence of a "hierarchy of truths," that some truths of the faith (as it is taught) are more central to the core of the faith than others. Believers must understand, for example, that assenting to the dogma of the Trinity is on a different level than abstaining from meat on Fridays during Lent. But these kinds of distinctions were not effectively made in the church before the council. After all, in this model those at the top *have* the truth, those at the bottom *receive* the truth—without question. To be fair, given the authoritarian nature of society in general before Vatican II, it is understandable that the church would be comfortable with such an approach to the faith. But, as discussed in chapter 1, just as children grow up and need reasons to see the value of living a certain way, the same holds true for the laity. For the *sensus fidelium* to serve as a living and powerful force in the whole body of Christ, the laity must be offered a solid theological foundation for the faith. We are reminded of the quote from John Henry Newman regarding the theological formation of the laity: "I want a laity, not arrogant,…but men who know their religion, who enter into it,…who know their creed so well, that they can give an account of it…."[15]

In the same vein, most laypersons before Vatican II would not have been aware of the distinction between infallible and noninfallible teaching. In 1953, Yves Congar was concerned about the problem of "creeping infallibility," a situation in which there was a growing tendency on the part of the laity to regard any and all church teaching as infallible.[16]

A laity without a sound religious education was the rule rather than the exception before Vatican II. One other component of this sound education is the formation of a correct conscience. The church has always taught—at least in principle—the centrality of individual conscience. The theologians we have considered knew the important role of conscience in the act of faith. They knew, too, the danger of imposing from on high a collective and frequently ill-informed conscience on the faithful. Prompted by the ecclesial atmosphere in his day—Vatican I's formal articulation of the teaching on infallibility—John Henry Newman was absolutely committed to the critical role of conscience and the freedom of theological investigation.[17] Given his own recent conversion to Catholicism and his dismay over the articulation regarding papal infallibility at the First Vatican Council (1869–70), Newman claimed that he would "join with the best of men in drinking to the health of the pope—but of conscience first."[18] And, in our discussion of Karl Rahner's theological anthropology, that humans are by nature called to a supernatural end, it becomes clear that every believer is a "budding" theologian, urged on by a desire to know and understand what is accepted in faith. This cannot be achieved without a correctly informed conscience.[19]

The Law of Incarnation

Between 1937 and 1942, the biblical concept of the church as the people of God was becoming clearly established in Catholic theology. This rediscovery was made by the theologians who were attempting to go beyond the hierarchical and juridical focus that had been the prevailing understanding in ecclesiology. Even as early as 1922, in his book *The Church and the Catholic*, Romano Guardini was claiming that the church was awakening in the hearts of believers. For him, the church was not primarily a juridical, institutional structure, but "above all, the body of Christ...a place where Christ still lives and acts in the world."[20]

This same theme was taken up by M.-D. Chenu, who claimed that "the mystery of Christ is always in act...by an immanent presence in the community of his body."[21] This law of incarnation was a central theme in Chenu's theology and serves as another element in the development of a theology of the laity in the church. Reading the "signs of the times" became one of the mantras at Vatican II, and Chenu, many years before the council, was claiming that the whole church is called to this task. His incarnational theology led him to view all members of the church as continuations of the incarnation and co-creators with God in the transformation of the world. As the laity rises to a new consciousness, "they become the field for new exigencies of incarnation"[22] of the presence of God in our midst.

At the Second Vatican Council, Bishop John J. Wright of Pittsburgh said, "The faithful have been waiting for 400 years for a positive conciliar statement on the place, dignity and vocation of the layman."[23]

We turn now to examine Vatican II's response to the place, dignity, and vocation of the laity.

The Hour of the Laity

In 1906, Pope Pius X made the following statement in his encyclical *Vehementer nos* (On the French Law of Separation):

> In the hierarchy alone reside the power and authority necessary to move and direct all the members of the society to its end. As to the many (the laity) they have no other right than to let themselves be guided and so follow their pastors in docility.[24]

In 1988, Pope John Paul II observed:

> The lay faithful participate in the life of the church not only in exercising their tasks and charisms but also in many other ways.[25]

In the eight decades separating these two very different observations on the laity, a radical development had occurred regarding the role of the layperson in the church. There had been some progress made early in the twentieth century with regard to the apostolate of the laity. Pope Pius XI (1922–39) had encouraged the faithful who were participating in various forms of Catholic Action. In 1946, Pope Pius XII told the College of Cardinals that the laity "are the church."[26] Still, even these attempts failed to offer an authentic apostolate for the layperson, an apostolate that was not simply a "sharing" in the hierarchy's mission in the church. As we have seen, many seeds were being sown during the twentieth century by those theologians who had a broader vision of the layperson's place in the church. But, it would be at the Second Vatican Council that the hour of the laity would ultimately be recognized.

Vatican II Opens the Door

Vatican II was the first ecumenical council in the history of the church to deal with the topic of the laity. In fact, the term *layman* occurs 206 times in the council's documents, and all the references are favorable. As we read through the documents, we find three in particular that contribute to a renewed understanding of the vocation of the laity in the church: *Lumen Gentium, Gaudium et Spes,* and *Apostolicam Actuositatem.*

When we read these documents, we find that the council fathers made some critical adjustments to the preconciliar understanding of the layperson in the church. We can also discern some of the key topics that would affect an authentic theology of the laity: the significance of baptism; how the layperson is defined; the concept of the priesthood of the faithful; the *sensus fidelium* and its role; the realm of the lay apostolate—spiritual or secular; the relationship of the laity to the hierarchy.

In the years between John XXIII's announcement of the council in 1959 and its opening in 1962, there had been a frenzied period of preparation. The laity had not enjoyed any major participation during this period, but they did have a number of bishops who had a genuine sense of the needs of the laity and of their potential mission in the church. Leon Cardinal Joseph Suenens was one such bishop. At the council, he claimed:

> We need a major declaration on the role of the laity in the church—all we have at present are three lines in the articles of canon law! A schema *de laicis* (on the laity) has been drafted, but it needs to be rewritten with greater breath and soul....An important statement should be drafted...recognizing the rights and obligations of lay people by virtue of their baptism.[27]

Apostolicam Actuositatem, the Decree on the Apostolate of the Laity, would ultimately be promulgated and it was devoted entirely to the place of the laity in the church. However, this document had its roots in *Lumen Gentium*, especially in chapter 4, where we find the beginnings of a theological foundation for the lay apostolate. So, we begin with some insights from *Lumen Gentium*.

Lumen Gentium

This Dogmatic Constitution on the Church had undergone quite a difficult journey before it was officially promulgated on November 21, 1964. The competing models of church—pyramid versus communion—in the minds of the council fathers is one reason for the difficulty. As stated earlier, one's theology of church will yield a theology of the laity. A careful reading of this document reveals evidence of these very different theologies of church. Still, in chapter 4 of *Lumen Gentium* on the laity, we do find a statement that would ultimately pave the way for significant developments for the laity in the church. Referring back to chapter 2 in the document, which dealt with the people of God, the council fathers state: "Everything that has been said above concerning the people of God is intended for the laity, religious and clergy alike."[28] Further along, in chapter 5, we find another assertion that would alter the way we viewed the laity and support a communitarian model of being church. "Therefore, in the church, everyone whether belonging to the hierarchy, or being cared for by it, is called to holiness."[29] And in the next article: "Thus it is evident to everyone, that the faithful of Christ of whatever rank or status, are called to the fullness of Christian life and to the perfection of charity."[30] *Lumen Gentium* recognizes the various classes and duties of life, but insists that "holiness is one."[31] This universal call to holiness was a remarkable moment for the church. In the preconciliar period, with its sharp division between the clergy and the laity, it was simply assumed that priests and nuns were expected to attain to a higher level of graced perfection. Our expectations regarding the spiritual development of the layperson were much lower. But the council fathers dismissed this division, claiming that by virtue of our baptism, each member is called to holiness. "The followers of Christ are called by God....They are justified in the Lord Jesus, because in the baptism of faith they truly become sons of God and sharers in the divine nature. In this way they are really made holy."[32] Hence, this universal call is lived out in various ways, in different vocations, in many ministries. Still, our baptism places us in communion with each other.

The theological implications of this universal call to holiness by virtue of our baptism would have far-reaching effects on the way the laity would henceforth be viewed. The underlying point, made as we have seen by many theologians in the decades prior to the council, is this: Through baptism, each member of the church receives the Holy Spirit, a reception that makes us one.

Vatican II had retrieved a New Testament position, one that emphasized the importance of the church as a communion of grace rather than that of institution. Such a view was a central theme in Yves Congar's theology. He maintained that the church grows through the many contributions of all the members. In this way, the church benefits from the fullness of the gifts of the Holy Spirit.[33]

As we have already noted, Cardinal Suenens was one the laity's greatest proponents at the council. He maintained that this rediscovery of the entire people of God as a single reality was one of the most fruitful seeds of Vatican II. And that it implied, among other things, a coresponsibility for each member of the church. In Suenens's mind, the great proclamation from the Letter to the Ephesians, "One Lord, one faith, one baptism,"[34] had finally been understood in the church.[35] As we would come to see, this emphasis on Christian baptism would reveal many riches for lay activity in the church.

Priesthood of the Faithful

For one thing, our rediscovery of the privileges accorded to all through baptism brought forward a principle that had a long history in the church's tradition, but had been for too long forgotten: the priesthood of the faithful. Before discussing this principle, one point should be made. *Lumen Gentium* offered a clear definition of the laity: "The term…is here understood to mean all the faithful except those in holy orders and those in the state of religious life specially approved by the church."[36] There is no need to view this definition as devaluing the status of the layperson in any way. The document goes on to see the laity as fully constituted among the whole people of God by virtue of their baptism[37] and points to the fact that the laity share in the priestly, prophetic, and kingly functions of Christ.[38] In their priestly role, through their works, prayers, and acts of worship, the laity consecrate the world to God.[39] By their example and witness, they enlighten those who seek the truth, thereby fulfilling their prophetic role.[40] Finally, by serving Christ in their brothers and sisters they lead them to the king for whom to serve is to reign.[41]

With regard to the idea of "priesthood," *Lumen Gentium* does make a distinction between the priesthood of the faithful and the ministerial priesthood (those who are ordained), claiming that the two differ in essence and not only in degree,[42] but all members share the essential responsibilities of praying, of bearing witness to Christ, of proclaiming Christ to all.[43] However, in the years before Vatican II this distinction between the ordained priesthood and the priesthood of the faithful also resulted in a distinction regarding the realm in which each group would practice their ministry. The "sacred" realm was reserved for the clergy, and the "secular" was the appropriate domain for the activity of the laity. Even though *Lumen Gentium* does make references to the specifically secular nature of the lay apostolate, it also acknowledges that this apostolate is "a participation in the salvific mission of the church itself"[44] and that they are "commissioned by the Lord himself."[45] This is a very important point. For so long, the lay apostolate was seen as a "sharing" in a ministry that belonged to the hierarchy. The laity had been viewed as "helpmates" to the hierarchy. *Lumen Gentium*

73

changes this perception. The ministry is not something "given" to them by the hierarchy. Rather, it is something they are called to by their God, by virtue of their baptism. This was a remarkable and defining moment for the laity in the church. They are finally recognized as having a ministry of their own, one that is truly vital to the well-being of the church.

Gifted with the Same Spirit

We have already touched upon another theological principle that flows from the privileges associated with the giving of the Holy Spirit: the *sensus fidelium*. Faithful to the New Testament and following the insights offered by their theological colleagues in the years leading up to Vatican II, the council fathers included this very important element in their discussion of the laity. This concept not only respects the significance of the laity's full membership in the church, but it also acknowledges the role they play in the actual development and reception of church teaching.

Earlier, we spoke about John Henry Newman's belief that the faithful should be consulted in matters of faith and doctrine. How gratified he would have been to read the following teaching from *Lumen Gentium*:

> The entire body of the faithful, anointed as they are by the Holy One, cannot err in matters of belief. They manifest this special property by means of the whole peoples' supernatural discernment in matters of faith when from the bishops down to the last of the lay faithful they show universal agreement in matters of faith and morals. That discernment...is aroused and sustained by the Spirit of truth.[46]

At the church's very first council, the Council of Jerusalem, we saw that a decision was made "with the consent of the whole church."[47] This same principle is taken up again and agreed to at the Second Vatican Council. The "sense of the faithful" provides this certitude only when the whole church participates. This is because the very Spirit who inspires a teaching of the hierarchy is the very same Spirit who receives the teaching in the members. The Spirit cannot contradict itself.

The implications of this principle are significant. In our next chapter, we examine *Lumen Gentium* in greater depth, and we also add to our discussion of "reception" (how the members receive a particular teaching, how they perceive its truthfulness). But, for now, it seems that *Lumen Gentium* has made a very clear point. The church can no longer justify viewing the laity as mere spectators in the mission and teaching of the church. The laity have an active role in the development of doctrine. They do not simply receive the truth from above—rather, they collaborate with the official teaching body of the church. This privilege is a result of "the giving of the Spirit" at baptism.

Relationship between the Laity and the Hierarchy

Before moving on to our next document, we need to address another element of *Lumen Gentium*'s treatment of the laity: their relationship to the hierarchy. Knowing the kind of relationship that prevailed in the preconciliar period, one marked by the laity's obedience, docility, and passivity, what could we expect now...given the council's acknowledgment that we are all the people of God? As theologian Richard McBrien has noted, "The traditional division of labor—clergy in the sacristy and laity in the world—is artificial and even false."[48] And, we are reminded of John Henry Newman, who maintained that the Magisterium (the official teaching body of the church) was indeed needed for the passing on of the faith. But Newman also maintained that the Magisterium never operated alone.[49]

So, what kind of laity-hierarchy relationship is envisioned by the council fathers? Given the laity's long journey to have their voice heard in the church, *Lumen Gentium* provides a remarkable moment in that journey. The document does speak of the need for the laity "to accept in Christian obedience the decisions of their spiritual shepherds."[50] It also encourages the laity to pray for their spiritual leaders.[51]

But article 37 also contains some suggestions that would come as a surprise, given the status of the layperson prior to Vatican II. *Lumen Gentium* claims that the laity are "by reason of their knowledge, competence or outstanding ability,...permitted and sometimes even obliged to express their opinion on those things which concern the good of the church."[52] And, with regard to the hierarchy's response to the laity's "new-found" voice, we read:

> Let the spiritual shepherds recognize and promote the dignity as well as the responsibility of the laity in the church....Let them encourage lay people so that they may undertake tasks on their own initiative....A great many wonderful things are to be hoped for from this dialogue...in the laity,...a sense of responsibility....(The hierarchy) aided by the experience of the laity, can more clearly...come to decisions regarding both spiritual and temporal matters. In this way, the whole church, strengthened by each one of its members, may more effectively fulfill its mission for the life of the world.[53]

Indeed, the laity had finally received very positive official recognition. We know that at the time, there were some council fathers who were not pleased by the privileges, rights, and obligations accorded to the laity at Vatican II. Cardinal Ernesto Ruffini, one of the Curia cardinals, "objected to the idea that the...spiritual gifts, so important to St. Paul (1 Corinthians 12:14) were still widespread in the church (and argued) that today they were very rare."[54] It would appear that these bishops were far more comfortable with the preconciliar approach and feared that such recognition of the laity would take away from the centralization enjoyed by Rome and domination exercised by some bishops in the life of the church. As to how *Lumen Gentium's* statements on the laity-hierarchy relationship would be played out in "real time" in the months and years to follow...well, that is a subject for another author and another book to examine. For our purposes, it is clear that the council fathers were truly opening the door for the potential "age of the layperson" in the church.

Gaudium et Spes

Of the sixteen documents produced at Vatican II, two were devoted to the study of the church: *Lumen Gentium* and *Gaudium et Spes*. The first was the "dogmatic" constitution on the church and the latter was the "pastoral" constitution. With regard to the term *pastoral,* Yves Congar has pointed out, "A pastoral approach is not without doctrine....It intends to present the truth of salvation in a way which is close to men and women of today and which accepts their difficulties and tries to answer their questions."[55]

As the final document to be promulgated at the council on December 7, 1965, *Gaudium et Spes* takes for granted and builds on what has already been said in the other documents. As we saw in our earlier treatment of the church-world relationship, *Gaudium et Spes* clearly places the church *in* the world. This makes the apostolate of the laity all the more significant. In fact, *Gaudium et Spes* has been referred to as "the bible of the lay apostolate."[56]

A Theology of the Actual

In a previous discussion, we examined *Gaudium et Spes* in light of one of the paradigm shifts that changed the way we did theology. That was a shift in methodology—from deductive to inductive. Evidence of this approach is found in the focal point of the document, as stated in article 2: "Therefore, the council focuses its attention on the world of men, the whole human family along with the sum of those realities in the midst of which it lives."[57] We have come to know Cardinal Suenens, one of the most important figures at Vatican II and clearly a key player in the council's treatment of the laity. In his writings, Suenens had called for "a theology of the actual."[58] He believed that since the laity are so much a part of "the world," they are more able to find a way of truly speaking to the world. Of course, the laity's voice will only be heard if their lives are a living witness to the gospel. The drafters of *Gaudium et Spes* were keenly aware of a split that can occur between religious concerns and earthly affairs. They address Christians as citizens of two cities—the sacred and the secular—and advise them:

They are mistaken who, knowing that we have here no abiding city but seek one which is to come, think that they may therefore shirk their earthly responsibilities....Nor are they any less wide of the mark who think that religion consists in acts of worship alone...and who imagine they can plunge themselves into earthly affairs in such a way as to imply that these are...divorced from the religious life. This split between the faith which many profess and their daily lives deserves to be counted among the more serious errors of our age.[59]

This "divorce" between religion and one's daily life was becoming more and more apparent in the years before Vatican II, and it had been addressed by a number of theologians. In 1939, Romano Guardini wrote *The World and the Person*, in which he offered insights on how to live as a Christian in the modern age. Guardini was convinced that Christian witness meant providing the world with opportunities to meet the living Christ.[60] This theme of authentic witness is espoused as well by John Henry Newman and Yves Congar. Both were convinced that the laity needed to make the Christian story their own and evangelize "the world" by their witness.[61]

This "theology of the actual" is indeed an appropriate context in which to understand *Gaudium et Spes* and one that had been suggested for many years before the council by theologians such as Yves Congar, who claimed that the decisive factor for the laity "is determined by their *situation in the world*....They have to give glory to God, not by withholding themselves from that work, but precisely *in* it and *through* it."[62]

Theologically Prepared for the Mission

However, in order for the laity to assume their rightful place in the mission of the church, in order that they might indeed provide opportunities for the world to meet the living Christ, there must be an opportunity for the laity to grow in their understanding of the Christian story.

Lay participation in formal theology programs was rare in the years leading up to the council. This was considered the domain of the clergy. Vatican II proposed a change that would significantly improve the laity's involvement in such programs. In the section discussing some urgent duties of Christians with regard to culture, *Gaudium et Spes* states:

> It is to be hoped that many of the laity will receive a sufficient formation in the sacred sciences and that some will dedicate themselves professionally to these studies....In order that they may fulfill their function, let it be recognized that all the faithful, whether clerics or laity, possess a lawful freedom of inquiry, freedom of thought and of expressing their mind with humility and fortitude in those matters on which they enjoy competence.[63]

And, continuing to draw on the discussion of the rights and responsibilities of the laity, as outlined in *Lumen Gentium*, this document offers important advice and encouragement to the laity when it claims:

> Let the layman not imagine that his pastors are always such experts, that to every problem which arises, however complicated, they can readily give him a concrete solution, or even that such is their mission....Since they have an active role to play in the whole life of the church, laymen are not only bound to penetrate the world with a Christian spirit, but are also called to be witnesses to Christ in all things in the midst of human society.[64]

Lumen Gentium had provided the foundation for many of the insights that would be "fleshed out," so to speak, in *Gaudium et Spes*'s treatment of the laity. *Apostolicam Actuositatem* would rely on *Lumen Gentium* as well. We turn now to a discussion of this document's contribution to the lay vocation in the church.

Apostolicam Actuositatem

This Decree on the Apostolate of Lay People was promulgated on November 18, 1965, during the final session of the Second Vatican Council. It passed with 2,340 votes in the affirmative, 6 in the negative. It was the only council document devoted entirely to the laity in the church.

This document underwent many stages, particularly during meetings that were held in between the formal sessions of Vatican II. These discussions provided moments of high drama and heated tension between those who favored Roman centralization and/or the virtual monopoly of leadership roles by the local bishops, not yet willing to yield any significant "power" to the laity in the church, and those who believed that the New Testament suggested a more meaningful role for the layperson, by virtue of their baptism. Fortunately, this latter group had the support of the two popes who served during the council. In 1963, shortly before he died, Pope John XXIII issued his encyclical, *Pacem in Terris* (Peace on Earth). In it, he claimed that "Christians were not to look to human institutions for salvation and protection but were to be active in them as the incorruptible leaven of Christian life."[65] After John XXIII's death in June 1963, Giovanni Battista Montini was elected pope, taking the name of Pope Paul VI. As archbishop of Milan, Montini had been a very strong advocate of the laity. As the pope who would oversee the remaining sessions of Vatican II, he decided to invite lay auditors to the council, a decision that was made public on September 14, 1963.[66]

Perhaps the statement that best set the tone for this decree on the laity was the one made by Cardinal Cento, who presented the draft of *Apostolicam Actuositatem* to the council fathers in 1964: "It is the heart of this text, and our deepest desire, that all the baptized may become aware that no one can be a genuine Christian until he or she thinks of themselves as an apostle; the manifestation of such an awareness would be the greatest triumph of Vatican Council II."[67]

An Ecclesiology of the People of God

Apostolicam Actuositatem opens with a significant declaration: "The apostolate of the laity derives from their Christian vocation and the church can never be without it."[68] It announced that the mission of the laity is grounded in their baptism, and this mission is exercised both in the church and in the world.[69] As such, each has received gifts—charisms—from the Holy Spirit that prepare the faithful for their apostolate: to build up the body of Christ. Each is a full member of the people of God.

Drawing on *Lumen Gentium*'s discussion of the rights and responsibilities of the whole people of God, the decree adds, "Bishops, pastors of parishes and other priests...should keep in mind that the right and duty to exercise this apostolate is common to all the faithful, both clergy and laity, and that the laity also have their own roles in building up the church."[70] This last emphasis on the laity having "their own roles" is important. *Apostolicam Actuositatem* locates the apostolate of the laity in a theology of charisms, gifts of the Holy Spirit. As Karl Rahner has pointed out, if the whole people of God are gifted by the Spirit, then the hierarchy cannot administer a centralized system where individuals have no initiative.[71] Rahner emphasized that the laity not only possess charisms, but that they receive them for the same purpose as the hierarchy: "to enable them to contribute toward making the church a living sign of Christ in the world."[72] In this regard, the decree calls for a relationship of mutual esteem and respect between the laity and the hierarchy.[73]

Preparation to Be an Apostle

The New Testament tells us, "Always be ready to make your defense to anyone who demands an accounting for the hope that is in you."[74] This responsibility extends to the whole people of God. *Apostolicam Actuositatem* repeats this command, exhorting the laity "to be more diligent in doing what they can to explain, defend and properly apply Christian principles to the problems of our era in accordance with the mind of the church."[75] We are reminded of the teaching of our previously discussed council documents that pointed to the need for solid theological education of the laity. As the familiar saying goes, "We cannot give what we do not have." The whole people of God must come to own the Christian story and witness to that story by their lives. Only then can they truly be the leaven in the modern world. Only then can they offer an effective apostolate for the mission of the church. Only then can they be considered "apostles" with an apostolate of their own.

Vatican II finally acknowledged what so many already knew in the years leading up to the council: that we are all the people of God by virtue of our baptism, that we all have gifts to use in the mission of the church. Like no previous council in the history of the church, Vatican II invited the laity to assume their rightful place and contribute to the transformation of the world.

Conclusion

We have seen that in the years leading up to the Second Vatican Council, the church focused more on the centrality of the clergy and marginalized the place of the layperson in ecclesial matters.

We have also seen that through their "return to the sources," theologians came to see that this division between clergy and laity was a development that found no home in the New Testament. These theologians would come to realize that "the giving of the Holy Spirit" to all believers in baptism could become the foundation for an authentic theology of the laity in the church.

The fruits of their labors would come to pass at Vatican II, where certain key elements would be incorporated into the council's treatment of the laity: the meaning of Christian baptism, the *sensus fidelium*, the priesthood of the faithful, the appropriate realm for the lay apostolate, and the proper relationship of the laity to the hierarchy and vice versa.

Ultimately, Vatican II came to see the church as a communion of grace rather than that of institution—focusing on a theology of charisms that would understand the church as "the people of God," a diversity of ministries, but a unity of mission.

Some of the theologians who had spent so many years working toward this moment lived long enough to see their theological aspirations fulfilled at Vatican II. Yves Congar was one of them. Reporting from Rome during the second session of the council, he wrote, "It is with intense joy that I have witnessed with fine results a maturing theology of the laity....Emphasis has been laid on the fundamental equality of all in Christian dignity."[76]

It should be noted that there are those who are not quite as positive in their evaluation of Vatican II's treatment of the laity.[77] Still, based on our reading of the documents, we would prefer to accept Congar's position, stated in a 1964 interview: "Seeds planted today will give their fruit later, in thirty to fifty years."[78] Vatican II set the stage for the "age of the layperson" in the church. Time will tell if and how far these seeds will indeed bear fruit.

4

THE CHURCH LOOKS
AT ITSELF

From Vatican I to Vatican II

Vatican II was a council *of* the church *about* the church. Hence, it seems fitting to conclude our study of the road to Vatican II with a discussion of the church's self-understanding, seen through the lens of *Lumen Gentium*, the Dogmatic Constitution on the Church.

Lumen Gentium was promulgated in November 1964. It can be considered the centerpiece of the sixteen documents of Vatican II because it contains many of the key theological achievements of the council. Overall, the document announced a major transition that was taking place in the church's self-understanding—a transition from a hierarchical model to a communitarian model. But *Lumen Gentium* also revealed remarkable insights into specific concerns that touch upon the meaning of church, such as the church as the people of God, the church as the sacrament of salvation, the church as mystery, collegiality in the church's leadership, the significance of the local church and its relationship to the universal church, the universal call to holiness for all members of the church, and the relationship between the Magisterium and the faithful. Indeed, *Lumen Gentium* was intended "to describe the church's life *ad intra*, that is to say its nature, its relationship to revelation, its inner structures, ministries, and general vocation."[1]

However, in order to truly appreciate this document, one must go back in time to the First Vatican Council (1869–70), called by Pope Pius IX. Most commentators would agree that it is the debate and doctrine of papal infallibility and jurisdiction that have become synonymous with Vatican I. When one reads the accounts of the infallibility debates at that council, it is hard not to be discouraged. Some seven hundred bishops came together at Vatican I; among them was a minority who fought against the move to define infallibility, concerned about the historical and theological problems it would raise. One theologian at the council, Dominican Cardinal Guidi, suggested "a formula that would speak of the pope's doctrinal definitions rather than of the infallibility of the pope—a phrase that connoted an idea of his personal infallibility." His suggestion would include the need for the pope to give serious consideration to tradition, which would have involved consulting with his bishops. This proposal did not sit well with Pius IX, who shouted back, *"Tradizione! La tradizione son' io!"* ("Tradition! I am Tradition!")[2] The debate continued, but in the end the minority voice was defeated and Vatican I declared that "definitions of the Roman Pontiffs...were of themselves irreformable."[3]

Pius IX died in 1878 but, clearly, his influence would be felt by the twentieth-century church. As Vatican affairs writer Peter Hebblethwaite has said, "It matters very much who is pope. Each pope makes his own distinctive contribution."[4]

By the middle of the twentieth century, the Catholic Church was in what we might call a state of siege mentality:

> Deeply suspicious of the modern world, Catholic scholarship had been crippled by the atmosphere of suspicion and distrust that followed the Modernist Crisis at the beginning of the twentieth century. Books by Catholic authors were rarely published without a review by ecclesiastical authorities....The only really acceptable model for theology was that of the dogmatic manuals of the Roman schools. Rather than asking new questions and investigating biblical and historical sources, this textbook theology demonstrated traditional positions by citing biblical prooftexts and...papal and conciliar teachings.[5]

The prevailing model of the church at the time was the hierarchical model, also referred to as the "pyramid" model. We touched on this model in chapter 3. In this model, church members are viewed in a "rank-and-file" manner—pope at the top, followed by clergy, religious men and women, and the laity. This model had serious theological implications, and anyone schooled in the Catholic faith before Vatican II would be very much aware of those implications. Truth comes from the top and is received by the members below. Dialogue is not an option. Priests, religious brothers, and nuns were thought to be holier than the laity by virtue of their religious calling. (Obviously the clergy abuse scandals that came to light in recent years have shown the error of this assumption.) The relationship of the pope to his bishops was similar to that of a CEO and his company. Here again, one can see the influence of Pius IX: "I am Tradition!" It is a far cry from the New Testament model of Jesus washing the feet of his disciples at the Last Supper. The notion of collegiality, a concept used by Vatican II to describe the common responsibility that the whole episcopal body has with regard to the exercise of authority and teaching in the church, is virtually nonexistent in the pyramid model. And, as far as the laity is concerned, it was clear that church officials viewed the laity as "helpers" of the hierarchy and not in possession of a distinct mission of their own.

This model of church, with such a strong emphasis on the institution, with many privileges accorded to those with priestly and religious vocations, with its emphasis on rules and rituals, did not find a home in the New Testament, where we find the birth of the church. To be fair, a survey of church history, especially since the Reformation, indicates how this hierarchical model came to be. The popes of the eighteenth and nineteenth centuries had been battling the forces of the modern world. Somehow they came to believe that the way for the church to avoid future crises was to insulate itself behind a power structure that would be self-sufficient, that would have all the answers. But, as we have seen in the previous chapters, there were those prophets in our midst who believed that this model of church was in need of renewal and reform…that this model was so far away from that of the early church, where leadership existed for service and to help maintain proper order and teaching; where to be a member of the community was to be recognized by the love one had for others; where rules and laws, though important, were not the primary goal in the way of discipleship; where it was recognized that to be church was to truly make God present in the world...to be the sacrament of salvation. These are some of the aspects our theologians came to understand when they returned to the sources of the faith.

Changing the Unchangeable

In the years between Vatican I and Vatican II, one of the most treasured characteristics of the church was seen to be its "immutability," the belief that the church and the faith were timeless, eternal realities that do not change. This was a central component of the classicist worldview, which we discussed in chapter 1.

The dramatic theological journey that took place between the two councils has been a focal point of this book. Many prophets contributed along the way and frequently paid a very dear price for their contributions. In the field of ecclesiology, Yves Congar was one of the central figures, if not *the* central figure on the road to Vatican II. Congar and his theological colleagues have helped us to understand how we moved from a Pius IX at Vatican I to a John XXIII at Vatican II, from a church that understood itself primarily as a hierarchical institution to a church understood as a communion.

Once, during an interview, Congar was asked to comment on decisive turning points in the history of the church.[6] In response, Congar claimed that in his mind the most important turning point occurred in the eleventh century in the papacy of Gregory VII. This pope instituted a reform in the church to address a particular problem —the relationship between the spiritual authority at the time, the pope, and the civil authority, King Henry IV. But, in the course of this reform, Gregory VII made the church itself into a legal institution, and in the end papal power became the foundation for everything. The aspect of legality came to be more significant than sacramentality. Congar sees this as a fateful development, because

> it contributed to this conceptual legalization and to the transition from the idea of a spiritual communion arising out of the Eucharist (which was the dominant model during the first millennium) to the idea of a society, a

hierarchical, institutional church society (which then became the prevailing model in the second millennium.)[7]

Congar acknowledged that, of course, in a certain sense the church is a society, but a true theology of church must be rooted, first and foremost, in the concept of communion.

In the course of the second millennium, we do see the church becoming more and more legalistic, juridical, and clericalistic. Theologian Karl Rahner also wrote about this unfortunate development in ecclesiology. In his pre–Vatican II writings, Rahner referred to the period that saw the papacies from Pius IX (1846–78) to Pius XII (1939–58) as the "age of Pian monolithism." (Years later, he would say that Vatican II broke the Pian mold.)[8] Rahner singled out three components that he believed characterized this "Pian monolithism": its emphasis on the unchangeable; the belief that the entire church should "look like" the church in Rome (for example, same liturgy, same discipline, same customs, and so on); and its belief that the absolute key to unity in the church is papal primacy. For Rahner, this model of church was, quite simply, an aberration.[9]

Just before the opening of the Second Vatican Council, Rahner wrote an article entitled "Thoughts on the Possibility of Belief Today,"[10] in which he discussed what he considered to be a mark of the church's sinfulness—the church's lack of trust in the Holy Spirit, a lack that Rahner claimed often manifested itself in a refusal to change.[11] He wrote, "It [the church] often places more value on the bureaucratic apparatus in the church than in the enthusiasm of the Spirit; it often loves the calm more than the storm, the old which has proved itself more than the new which is bold." And then, perhaps reflecting his own difficulties with the official church, Rahner added, "Often in the past, the church has in its office bearers wronged saints, thinkers, those who were painfully looking for an answer, or theologians—all of whom merely wanted to give their selfless service."[12] What becomes very clear from a reading of Rahner's preconciliar writings is that before John XXIII had called for an *aggiornamento*, Rahner himself was committed to the need for change in the church.[13]

Between Vatican I and Vatican II there were many voices calling for the church to move away from its practice of isolation, from its suspicious attitude toward the modern world, and from its legalistic, juridical approach to matters of faith. Despite these calls for change, the church of October 1958, when Angelo Roncalli ascended to the chair of Peter, "was defensive and immobile in the face of a rapidly changing world."[14]

But this was about to change. Vatican II would be the voice of this change, the voice of those prophets who had labored for so many years to bring the church into modernity and to restore a model of church found in the New Testament. We will see the results of their theological labors now as we turn to a discussion of *Lumen Gentium*, the Dogmatic Constitution on the Church, and discover how the church's self-understanding would change in this charter that was being written for the church of the third millennium.

Lumen Gentium: A Charter for Change

It is common knowledge that some of the documents that were put together during the preparation period for Vatican II were found unacceptable by the council fathers once the council began. This was especially true for the schema on the church. As one commentator noted, the preliminary schema referred to as schema 17, *De Ecclesia*, was "a summary of the pontifical teaching of the past one hundred and fifty years."[15] Overall, the criticisms of the language and concepts employed in this first draft were summed up by Bishop Emile de Smedt of Belgium, who criticized its triumphalism, clericalism, and its juridicism.[16] Perhaps the words of Cardinal Giovanni Montini, who would ascend to the papacy after the death of John XXIII in June 1963 as Pope Paul VI, best expressed the dissatisfaction of the council fathers with the initial schema on the church. His words also reflect the direction that many of the bishops hoped the council would take. Speaking in his diocese, Milan, on the feast of Saint Ambrose in December 1962, Montini stated these powerful words:

> Yesterday, the theme of the church seemed to be confined to the power of the pope. Today, it is extended to the episcopate, the religious, the laity, and the whole body of the church. Yesterday, we spoke of the rights of

the church by transferring the constitutive elements of civil society to the definition of [the church as] a perfect society. Today, we have discovered other realities in the church—the charisms of grace and holiness, for example —which cannot be defined by purely juridical ideas. Yesterday, we were above all interested in the external history of the church. Today, we are equally concerned with its inner life, brought to life by the presence of Christ in it.[17]

Montini was reflecting a critical shift that the church would undergo at Vatican II: we would see a transition from a *juridical* vision to a *theological* vision, and *Lumen Gentium* would be the herald of this transition. The original schema on the church with legalistic and militant language would, by November 1964, become *Lumen Gentium*, Light to the Nations. That light, of course, was the person of Jesus Christ.

This christological focus was central to the theology of Pope Paul VI. During his papal coronation speech on June 30, 1963, Paul VI said, "We hear them, these profound voices in the world. With God's help and the example of our predecessors, we will continue to offer untiringly to today's world the remedy for its ills, the answer to its appeals: Christ and his unfathomable riches."[18] And, when he opened the second session of Vatican II on September 29, 1963, he told his brother bishops—and the world, "There are three questions, essential in their extreme simplicity, but only one reply…Christ. Christ is our principle. Christ is our hope. Christ is our end."[19] Article 3 of *Lumen Gentium* closely echoes these words of Paul VI.

Cardinal Leon Suenens of Belgium proved to be one of the most significant voices at the council with regard to the document on the church. It was he who insisted that the document should first address the "inner life" of the church (*Ecclesia ad intra*), followed by a discussion of the "outer life" of the church (*Ecclesia ad extra*). And it was Cardinal Suenens who suggested the title *Lumen Gentium*.

When one compares the initial draft on the church, *De Ecclesia*, with the final version of *Lumen Gentium*, it becomes remarkably clear that *Lumen Gentium* was indeed a charter for change. Rather than opening with a chapter entitled "The Nature of the Church Militant," as did the first draft, *Lumen Gentium* begins with a chapter on the "mystery" of the church. As theologian Richard McBrien has noted, this was not simply an editorial move. Rather, "it reflects a fundamental shift in the way we understand the reality of the church."[20]

In the pages that follow, we examine this new understanding of church that *Lumen Gentium* reveals as mystery, communion, sacrament, eschatological, and try to understand the significant theological implications for a theology of the church. And, of course, we again meet those prophets who, for years, had been preparing the road for Vatican II. We shall see that the church had changed—from a static, unchanging timeless entity to a dynamic, pilgrim people on a journey to their ultimate destiny, the fullness of truth found only in God.

The Church Is a Mystery

One cannot help but be surprised by the language employed in *Lumen Gentium* to talk about the church, especially if one is familiar with the terms used in preconciliar official documents. Before Vatican II, Roman Catholicism often gave the impression that it had all the answers. It projected a grand certitude about all things related to the faith. This certitude frequently led those outside the church to accuse Roman Catholics of "ecclesiological triumphalism." Sadly enough, this accusation was often warranted. But here, in the very first chapter of a document in which the church reveals her own self-understanding, she uses the word *mystery*. In his speech, opening the second session of the council, Pope Paul VI gave us an insight into how the bishops wanted this term to be understood. The pope announced that the church was indeed a mystery: "a reality imbued with the hidden presence of God."[21]

As noted in chapter 2, Karl Rahner described mystery as "not that which I cannot know. (Rather) mystery is that which I cannot exhaust. I can never enclose it in definition."[22] The council fathers appear to be accepting Rahner's understanding, acknowledging that the church, a mystery filled with the hidden presence of God,

91

is beyond simple definition…just as God is beyond such definition. At best, one can only use descriptive images when speaking about these realities. Hence, we find the Bible speaking about God like an eagle, like a rock, like a mother who never forgets her child. So too with the church. Because it is indeed a mystery, one can never presume to capture it in a definition. Not surprisingly, *Lumen Gentium* does not provide a definition of the word *mystery*. However, in 1964, after a number of questions were raised regarding the meaning of the word, an official "interpretation" was given.[23] It explained that the word *mystery* "points to a transcendent, divine reality that has to do with salvation and that is in some sensible way revealed and manifested. The term, therefore, which is found in the Bible, is very suitable as a designation for the church."[24]

In choosing the word *mystery* as an image for the church, the council fathers were making an important point. In chapter 1, we discussed the need for theology to speak a language that gives life. The authors of *Lumen Gentium* chose to reject the language of the past—neoscholasticism—and to renew the faith with the language of the New Testament. As Walter Kasper has rightly pointed out:

> The Council's *aggiornamento* consisted in the fact that it again moved into the foreground the mystery of the church, which can only be grasped in faith, over against the one-sided concentration on the visible and hierarchical form of the church, which held sway during the previous three centuries.[25]

Choosing to describe the church as a mystery was one of the most important theological developments in Vatican II's contribution to the theology of church because "it recalls the church to a renewed contemplation of the presence of God within it,"[26] a God who is understood as triune communion. From the very beginning, *Lumen Gentium* links the mystery of the church to the ultimate mystery of the Holy Trinity, which is the source of its life:[27]

> The eternal Father, by a free and hidden plan of his own wisdom…planned to assemble in the holy church all those who would believe in Christ. Already from the

beginning of the world the foreshadowing of the church took place. It was prepared in a remarkable way throughout the history of the people of Israel and by means of the Old Covenant. In the present era of time the church was constituted and, by the outpouring of the Spirit, was made manifest....The Son, therefore, came, sent by the Father....To carry out the will of the Father, Christ inaugurated the kingdom of heaven on earth and revealed to us the mystery of that kingdom....When the work which the Father gave the Son to do on earth was accomplished, the Holy Spirit was sent on the day of Pentecost in order that he might continually sanctify the church....Thus, the church has been seen as a people made one with the unity of the Father, the Son and the Holy Spirit.[28]

Henri de Lubac was another of the "new theologians" who contributed to Vatican II's understanding of the church as mystery. In his book, *The Church: Paradox and Mystery*, de Lubac wrote:

The church is a mystery for all time out of man's grasp because, qualitatively, it is totally removed from all other objects of man's knowledge that might be mentioned. And yet, at the same time, it concerns us, touches us, acts in us, reveals us to ourselves.[29]

The mystery of the church, like the mystery of the incarnation, joins together the divine and the human. Or, as Romano Guardini described the relationship, the church's "real inner form" and its outer manifestations. Guardini was one of the very first of the "new theologians" to speak of the church as mystery. As early as 1907, influenced by his appreciation for the theology of the Tübingen School, especially that of Johann Adam Mohler, Guardini was referring to the church as "mysterious reality." (As far back as 1825, Mohler had been speaking about the church as a mystical communion.) One of the major strengths of Guardini's notion of church as mystery is its recovery of the ancient model of church—the recognition that the living Christ is the center of the believing community with the Holy Spirit as the source of unity.[30] Given the prevailing theology of church during Guardini's day, his insights emerge as all the more prophetic. It would be fair to say that one cannot understand the journey from the ecclesiology of Vatican I to the understanding of church in Vatican II without including a discussion of Guardini's vision of the church.[31]

In theological terms, a mystery is a reality that reveals God to us. Hence, it can be used interchangeably with the word *sacrament*.[32] Over the years there have been any number of definitions of the word *sacrament*. In the fifth century, Saint Augustine described sacraments as "visible signs of an invisible reality." The preconciliar catechism claimed that a sacrament "was an outward sign, instituted by Christ to give grace." Essentially, sacraments make God present. As such, Jesus Christ is the ultimate sacrament because, in a completely unique way, Jesus Christ makes God present to the world. As far back as 1938, Henri de Lubac prophetically extended this concept: "If Jesus Christ could be called the sacrament of God, then for us the church is the sacrament of Christ."[33]

The idea of the church as sacrament enjoyed a central place in the theology of *Lumen Gentium*. In the very first paragraph, we read, "The church is in Christ like a sacrament or as a sign and instrument both of a very closely knit union with God and of the unity of the whole human race." Then again, in chapter 7, we read, "Christ...rising from the dead...sent his life-giving Spirit upon his disciples and through him has established his body which is the church as the universal sacrament of salvation."[34]

The understanding of the church as the sacrament of salvation has been referred to as Karl Rahner's "trademark image" of the church.[35] When the council fathers decided to designate the church as a sacrament at the council, there were concerns on the part of non-Catholics. They feared that such a designation could lead the Roman Catholic Church to slip back into a kind of "ecclesiological triumphalism." This was clearly a problem in preconciliar times, but Rahner's approach avoids this problem. As early as 1934, Rahner had acknowledged that sinners continue to be members of the church. Such an acknowledgment prevents a notion of an "idealized" church.[36] *Lumen Gentium* echoes Rahner's understanding. After comparing the human and divine elements in the church to the mystery of the Incarnate Word, the document adds, "While Christ, holy, innocent and undefiled knew nothing of sin, but came to expiate only the sins of the people, the church, embracing in its bosom sinners, at the same time holy and always in need of being purified, always follows the way of penance and renewal."[37] In keeping with a cautious assertion of the church as a sacrament, the council fathers use the term *veluti* ("like") in their discussion in the first paragraph. The church is "like" a sacrament. The church sees herself as coming from Christ, and her authenticity in making God present in the world can only be understood in her total dependence on Christ, thereby avoiding any sense that the church in and of herself is an end in itself. It is important to note here a significant component of *Lumen Gentium*'s discussion of the church as the universal sacrament of salvation. As we shall see in a later discussion, the council fathers were not claiming that salvation was unavailable to those outside the Roman Catholic Church.

Still, even with this nuanced and very careful understanding of the church as the sacrament of salvation, it is difficult to convey to anyone who had not lived in the preconciliar period—a time when many Catholics still held that outside the church there could be no salvation—just how important this development was in the church's self-understanding. Church historian John O'Malley makes the point. He discusses the many changes that would come about as result of the council and claims, "Of all the changes...few were more profound in their implications than that there was 'salvation outside the church,' even outside Christianity." And, to make the point even further, O'Malley offers a quote from Pope Boniface VIII in 1302. The pope had asserted, "Furthermore, we declare, state, and define that it is absolutely necessary to salvation that every human creature be subject to the Roman Pontiff."[38] Few Roman Catholics living in the pre–Vatican II church would have imagined such a change in the church's theology of salvation. It would have been simply unthinkable for them. Perhaps Karl Rahner would not have been so surprised. In an article written shortly before the council, Rahner emphasized, "It was the Spirit who could move the church in directions which were not part of the church's planning."[39] Rahner's absolute trust in the power of the

Holy Spirit and the need for the church to be always open to the Spirit prompted him to make the following claim:

> The church is asked by God whether it has the courage to undertake an apostolic offensive into the future and therefore whether it has the necessary courage to show itself to the world in such an uninhibited way that no one could have the impression that the church goes on existing only as a relic from earlier times because it has not yet had enough time to die.[40]

In 1944, in a book on Saint Thomas Aquinas, the author wrote, "A theology which is no longer in tune with its time is a false theology."[41] Given the chance, Karl Rahner would probably have added, "A theology not listening to the Holy Spirit is a false theology."

In the New Testament, we read that "God desires everyone to be saved."[42] Given the developments in the field of interpreting the scriptures in the years since Pope Pius XII's encyclical *Divino Afflante Spiritu* (Inspired by the Holy Spirit) in 1943, the document that opened the door to a reading of the Bible using the tools of biblical criticism, the church was no longer approaching the Bible in a fundamentalist manner. But theologians knew that even though there may be historical inaccuracies in the Bible, there were no theological inaccuracies. Hence, the passage from 1 Timothy 2:4, describing God's desire that all be saved, presented serious questions for the biblical scholars. It must have a theological significance. The notion of the church as a sacrament at the council was intended to indicate the role of the church in the divine economy of salvation.[43] For years, theologians had been looking for ways that this "salvation for all" might occur. Needless to say, the ecumenical significance of such a breakthrough would be a development so many had hoped for. In this regard, grounded in the labors of men like Congar and Rahner in particular, *Lumen Gentium* made the following remarkable claim:

> But the plan of salvation also includes those who acknowledge the Creator. In the first place amongst these there are the Mohamedans, who, professing to

hold the faith of Abraham, along with us adore the one and merciful God....Nor is God distant from those who in shadows and images seek the unknown God, for it is he who gives to all men life and breath and all things, and as Savior wills that all men be saved. Those also can attain to salvation who through no fault of their own do not know the Gospel of Christ or his church, yet sincerely seek God and moved by grace strive by their deeds to do his will as it is known to them through the dictates of conscience. Nor does Divine Providence deny the helps necessary for salvation to those who, without blame on their part, have not yet arrived at an explicit knowledge of God and with his grace strive to live a good life. Whatever good or truth is found amongst them is looked upon by the church as a preparation for the Gospel.[44]

This incredible development in the church's thinking with regard to the question of who can be saved is echoed again in *Gaudium et Spes*, the document that would follow *Lumen Gentium* and work out the *Ecclesia ad extra* (relations of the church outside itself). In article 22 of *Gaudium et Spes*, the council fathers are writing about the wonderful gifts that are bestowed upon Christians due to their identification with the paschal mystery. Toward the conclusion of this article, we find one of the most remarkable statements in the council's documents:

All this holds true not only for Christians, but for all men of good will in whose hearts grace works in an unseen way. For, since Christ died for all men, and since the ultimate vocation of man is in fact one, and divine, we ought to believe that the Holy Spirit in a manner known to God offers to every man the possibility of being associated with this Paschal Mystery.[45]

The council fathers were affirming, on the one hand, that grace is absolutely necessary for salvation. On the other hand, in what must be considered a truly graced moment in the life of the

97

church, they were claiming that the possibility of salvation is universally available.[46]

In his opening address at the second session of the council, alluded to earlier, Pope Paul VI affirmed the idea of the church as a mystery. In that same address, he went on to say that precisely because it is a mystery, steeped in the presence of God, "it is always, therefore, possible to gain new and deeper insights into its nature."[47] Vatican II's teaching on the possibility of salvation for all of humanity is clearly one of these new and deeper insights.

We move now to another "deep insight" about the church's self-understanding at Vatican II—the church as *communio*.

The Church Is a Communion

Countless books and articles have been written about the Second Vatican Council. Not all of the commentators agree in their interpretations of the Council or of the sixteen documents produced by the council fathers. There is, however, consensus on one point. Representing this consensus, Hermann Pottmeyer proposed a common approach to interpreting Vatican II "based on the Council's invitation to make the church a *communio* and a sign of salvation to the world."[48]

The vision of the church as a "communion" is not new. Indeed, communion ecclesiology was the very first ecclesiology in the church, as revealed in the New Testament. In a recent book, theologian Dennis Doyle claims that "communion ecclesiology is an approach to understanding the church." Rather than focus on the church as institution, it emphasizes the sacramental and historical dimensions of the church. He notes that there are a number of versions of this ecclesiological approach but these generally contain four characteristic elements: (1) They involve a retrieval of an understanding of church that was presupposed by the Christians of the first millennium. (2) They emphasize the aspect of communion between human beings and God as opposed to the institutional elements of church. (3) They value the need for visible unity through a shared participation in the Eucharist. (4) They promote a dynamic interplay between unity and diversity in the church.[49]

These characteristics stand in stark contrast to the ecclesiology that prevailed in the minds of most Catholics prior to the Second Vatican Council. But as we have seen, Yves Congar, along with the other "new theologians," was truly committed to the value of returning to the sources—a return that would uncover a treasure of insights for him and for the church.

For one thing, a study of the New Testament would reveal that current structures in the church need not be taken as absolutes. That the later church looked back to the New Testament as characterized by unity does not erase the reality that one can find a multiplicity of voices in the New Testament communities—not a precise hierarchy of offices to be viewed as a permanent norm for the future of the church. What we find is a variety of forms of leadership that developed according to the needs of the early church.

Congar discovered another important insight in the New Testament, one that would make a major contribution to the work of the fathers at the council. That insight was the rediscovery of that branch of theology known as "pneumatology," the study of the Holy Spirit. Somehow, over the years the church had neglected the pneumatological dimension in ecclesiology. In order to have a balanced ecclesiology, we must acknowledge both the christological and the pneumatological components in the establishment of the church at the very beginning. This founding of the church was the result of the activity of Jesus of Nazareth (the historical Jesus), the risen Christ, and the Holy Spirit. Jesus called the apostles, the risen Christ commissioned them, and they were baptized in the Holy Spirit at Pentecost, the event that is the culmination of the divine activity in establishing the church. One cannot understand the founding of the church apart from the activity of the Holy Spirit, the Spirit referred to by Congar as "the co-founder of the church." So, an authentic ecclesiology is one that values both the christological dimension (the calling and commissioning of the first office holders in the church) as well as the pneumatological dimension (the activity of the Holy Spirit in the individual members). However, Roman Catholic ecclesiology has traditionally emphasized the christological dimension in the church's founding and, therefore, the significance of those who hold office in the church. Such an emphasis favors the institutional aspect of church and neglects the very legitimate role of the members who, like the first apostles, are baptized in the Holy Spirit. "In order to arrive at a genuinely Catholic vision of the church, both aspects must be grasped together."[50] This understanding of the need for a balanced ecclesiology is clearly the position taken by the Second Vatican Council in its Dogmatic Constitution on the Church, *Lumen Gentium*. Its teaching on the place of the laity in the church is just one example. The council fathers claim:

> The entire body of the faithful, anointed as they are by the Holy One, cannot err in matters of belief. They manifest this special property by means of the whole peoples' supernatural discernment in matters of faith when, from the bishops down to the last of the lay faithful, they show universal agreement in matters of faith and morals. That discernment…is aroused and sustained by the Spirit of truth.[51]

This was the position taken by Congar as well:

> (Congar) emphasized that the Spirit while always in harmony with the Christological nature of the church…still has a distinct role to play. For the church has an eschatological nature; it isn't finished yet; it is as yet imperfect and on a journey toward its fulfillment. For Congar, the Holy Spirit is available not just for the defense of the *status quo*; the Spirit has a role to play in bringing about structural reform.[52]

It has been noted that Vatican II was not creative in the sense of producing something out of nothing.[53] The transition from church as hierarchy to church as communion is the result of a variety of causes and influences. And the work of any given theologian is often built on those theologians who have gone before him or her. This was certainly the case with Yves Congar.

During the nineteenth century, that transition from hierarchy to communion was slowly taking place, and one of the great centers of this ecclesiological movement was the Tübingen School of Theology in Germany. Johann Adam Mohler (1796–1838) was one of its star pupils. He would provide the foundation for many of Congar's theological insights. Congar acknowledged that "in (Mohler), I found a source….What Mohler had done in the nineteenth century became for me an ideal…in the twentieth century."[54] Then again, in 1970, contributing to a volume honoring the Tübingen faculty, Congar wrote, "Mohler can even today be a vital source—that is what he was for me over forty years ago."[55]

Mohler was a patristic and medieval scholar and his studies led him to focus on the church as a community as well as on the inner reality of the life of grace. He is a central figure in the history of ecclesiology for three reasons:

> First, his early Spirit-centered understanding of the church…did have an influence in the twentieth century, most notably on Yves Congar. Second, his mature incarnation-centered ecclesiology was an important moment in the recovery of the image of the Mystical Body of Christ for the church; one can see its effect on Pius XII's *Mystici Corporis* (1943). But third and most importantly, the development of his ecclesiology in interaction with his Christology and theological anthropology gradually affected the way subsequent theologians understood the church. After him, the church was no longer the bearer of the mystery of the faith but was itself as aspect of that mystery.

The focus of ecclesiology moved away from questions about the institutional dimension of the church to discussions of the church's inner nature as well as the church's mission in the world in the plan of salvation.[56]

The concept of the church as communion yields a truly rich ecclesiology. It sees the Holy Spirit as the source of life in the church and promotes a renewed appreciation for the role of the charisms given to all the members by the Spirit for the building up of the church. The theological implications of a communion ecclesiology are many. The relationship between the local church and the universal church is one such implication, one that is closely related to the relationship between the pope and the bishops in the church. Chapter 3 of *Lumen Gentium* is dedicated to a discussion of the hierarchical structure of the church with a special focus on the episcopate, the body of bishops. This chapter prompted one of the most fiercely debated discussions at the council. As with most of the topics covered at Vatican II, two contrasting positions were at work. On the one side you had those bishops who were fearful about undermining papal primacy. The bishops on the other side had fears about papal absolutism.[57] This latter group had reason to be concerned. The prevailing mindset before Vatican II gave priority to the monarchical model of church governance over the collegial model. In this view, unity is achieved by the imposition of uniformity from above. As Hermann Pottmeyer has noted, the idea of "dialogue" as a method of communication in the church is new. The key words in the pre–Vatican II ecclesiology were *jurisdiction* and *obedience*.[58] Hence, the real challenge at Vatican II was to find a way to "reconcile the demands of unity with the requirements of diversity."[59]

Lumen Gentium tried to achieve that balance. It did affirm Vatican I's position on papal primacy, but it carefully situated it in a context that affirmed collegiality:

> Just as in the Gospel...St. Peter and the other apostles constitute one apostolic college, so in a similar way the Roman Pontiff, the successor of Peter, and the bishops, the successors of the apostles, are joined together. Indeed, the very ancient practice whereby bishops duly established in all parts of the world were in communion with one another and with the Bishop of Rome in a bond of unity, charity and peace, and also the councils assembled together....Both of these factors are already an indication of the collegiate character and aspect of the episcopal order; and the ecumenical councils held in the course of centuries are also manifest proof of that same character.

But, *Lumen Gentium* goes on to say:

> But the college or body of bishops has no authority unless it is understood together with the Roman Pontiff,

the successor of Peter as its head. The pope's power of primacy over all, both pastors and faithful, remains whole and intact....The order of bishops, which succeeds to the college of apostles and gives this apostolic body continued existence, is also the subject of supreme and full power over the universal church, provided we understand this body together with its head the Roman Pontiff and never without this head.[60]

In his commentary on this section of the document, Karl Rahner maintains that the chapter on the hierarchy does reflect a somewhat critical attitude with regard to a particular kind of Roman centralization, so prevalent in the decades before the council.[61] Such a development would be welcomed by those theologians who, over the years, had been critical of the overly centralized exercise of authority in the church. Between Vatican I and Vatican II, we find an exaggerated form of papal primacy and infallibility. During this time, "a monarchical 'one-man' rule and a kind of 'creeping infallibility' were all too evident,"[62] which prompted theologians like Congar to claim that "there is an ever present need for the criticism of the present historical forms of the church."[63] Both Congar and Chenu critiqued the ecclesiastical model of their day as "Baroque," characterized as being "anti-liberal, neoscholastic, and papalist."[64] And, Romano Guardini, in 1937, criticized the church for its "indolence, intolerance, tyranny and narrowness."[65] These were harsh words. But, in the minds of those theologians who were laboring to reform the church, fidelity to their church could not require a blind submission to authorities. One final criticism of the preconciliar exercise of authority comes from Congar, who asserted, "I eliminate at the start what amounts to be pure pontifical monarchy. It does not have consistent support either in the New Testament or in Christian antiquity."[66]

Vatican II's understanding of the hierarchy, especially its position on collegiality, would set the tone for another element in a communion ecclesiology mentioned earlier—that of the relationship between the local church and the universal church. The universal church is understood as a *communio ecclesiarum*, a fraternity of local churches brought together by the one Spirit.[67] *Lumen Gentium* holds that the local church makes present the church of Christ:

> A bishop marked with the fullness of the sacrament of Orders is the steward of the grace of the supreme priesthood, especially in the Eucharist, which he offers or causes to be offered, and by which the church continually lives and grows. This church of Christ is truly present in all legitimate local congregations of the faithful which, united with their pastors, are themselves called churches in the New Testament. For in their locality these are the new people called by God, in the Holy Spirit and in much fullness.

It was mentioned earlier that one challenge facing the council fathers was to find a way to preserve the unity of the church and still find a value in the diverse expressions of that unity. *Lumen Gentium* addresses this concern:

> This collegial union is apparent also in the mutual relations of the individual bishops with particular churches and with the universal church. The Roman Pontiff...is the perpetual and visible principle and foundation of unity of both the bishops and of the faithful. The individual bishops, however, are the visible principle and foundation of unity in their particular churches....The individual bishops represent each his own church, but all of them together and with the pope represent the entire church in the bond of peace, love, and unity.[68]

Given the preconciliar monolithic view of the church, *Lumen Gentium's* acknowledgment of the legitimacy of the local church is extremely important—remarkable as well. The importance of the local church can be traced back to the New Testament, where the various churches in Corinth, Ephesus, Rome, Jerusalem, and elsewhere were unified in those elements that were essential to the faith but often differed in the lived experience of that faith—for example, in discipline and liturgical expression. We know, for example, that some of the early local churches reflected a more institutional self-understanding while others, especially those influenced by the theology of Saint Paul, were clearly more charismatic. Still, they all confessed "one Lord, one faith, one baptism."[69]

The validity and significance of the local church had been of great interest in the writings of theologians in the years before the council. For them, the theological justification for the local church was rooted in their belief in the Holy Spirit, the soul of the church, the giver of charisms. Before Vatican II, a true appreciation of charisms was lacking in Roman Catholic ecclesiology, so much so that Congar claimed that "until recently, the Holy Spirit was rightly described as the forgotten God."[70] If the charisms were discussed, it was usually in the context of individual personal spirituality. But Congar believed that charisms were constitutive of the very essence of the church.[71]

The diversity inherent in a theology of the local church raises concerns for some who fear such diversity will disrupt unity in the church. Still, others recognize the value of legitimate diversity. From his very first encyclical, John XXIII acknowledged the genuine value of diverging opinions and the freedom of discussion, while still preserving the communion of faith.[72] And, in his study of the history of theology, Congar quotes Pope Benedict XV (1914–22), who asserted, "In matters which are not revelation, we must allow liberty of discussion."[73]

Dennis Doyle's book on communion ecclesiology offers an in-depth understanding of the church as communion. It includes a summary of the very important implications of the relationship between the local church and the universal church. First, this relationship promotes the validity of a diversity that can exist within a unity, a unity that must not simply be imposed from the top down. Second, it allows for the cultural adaptation of the gospel. We use the term *inculturation* in this regard. This concept is an acknowledgment of an inductive approach to evangelization in that it takes seriously the needs, questions, and circumstances of the local community. Finally, the relationship between the local church and the universal church carries significant implications for the exercise of authority in the church. In an attempt to move away from the pre–Vatican II monarchical exercise of papal authority, *Lumen*

Gentium stresses the role of the bishop as the leader of a given diocese. Hence, the bishop is not the vicar of the pope. He is the vicar
of Christ in the local church.[74] *Lumen Gentium* makes this clear:

> Bishops, as vicars and ambassadors of Christ, govern the
> particular churches entrusted to them by their counsel,
> exhortations, example, and even by their authority and
> sacred power....This power, which they personally exercise
> in Christ's name, is proper, ordinary and immediate....The
> pastoral office or the habitual and daily care of their sheep
> is entrusted to them completely; nor are they to be
> regarded as vicars of the Roman Pontiffs, for they exercise
> an authority that is proper to them, and are quite correctly
> called "prelates," heads of the people whom they govern.
> Their power, therefore, is not destroyed by the supreme
> and universal power, but on the contrary it is affirmed,
> strengthened and vindicated by it.[75]

One additional component of a communion ecclesiology should
be mentioned: the idea of reception. We touched on this topic in a
previous chapter but since it is a central concept in a *communio* theology, we revisit it here briefly. *Reception* is a theological term that
refers to "the process by which official teachings and decisions are
accepted, assimilated, and interpreted by the whole church."[76]
Reception of official teachings by the faithful is not simply a matter of obedience. Correctly understood, it involves a degree of
assent on the part of the faithful as well as the possibility of judgment. This concept did not enjoy a major role in pre–Vatican II
ecclesiology. For the most part, teachings were accepted, not
because of the intrinsic value of these teachings, but because of the
authority of those making them. When you have a system of juris-
dictional superiority, the principle of reception does not enjoy any
great significance. It is simply presumed that official teaching will
be accepted without hesitation in an expression of obedience.[77]
This understanding would undergo an important change at Vatican
II. As Congar had been insisting, "Reception includes a degree of
consent"[78] on the part of the faithful. In a communion ecclesiology,
respectful of the presence of the Holy Spirit in the community,

members have a responsibility in the ongoing search for truth. In fact, in the mind of one of Vatican II's leading figures, Cardinal Suenens, "coresponsibility was a central theme of the Council."[79] Suenens's claim is born out in *Lumen Gentium*:

> Christ, the great Prophet, who proclaimed the Kingdom of his Father both by the testimony of his life and the power of his words, continually fulfills his prophetic office until the complete manifestation of glory. He does this not only through the hierarchy who teach in his name and with his authority, but also through the laity whom he made his witnesses and to whom he gave understanding of the faith (*sensus fidei*).

And, again, two articles later:

> The laity have the right, as do all Christians, to receive in abundance from their spiritual shepherds the spiritual goods of the church....They are...permitted and sometimes even obliged to express their opinion on those things which concern the good of the church....A great many wonderful things are to be hoped for from this familiar dialogue between the laity and their spiritual leaders; in the laity a strengthened sense of personal responsibility; a renewed enthusiasm....The latter, on the other hand, aided by the experience of the laity, can more clearly and more incisively come to decisions regarding both spiritual and temporal matters. In this way, the whole church, strengthened by each one of its members, may more effectively fulfill his mission for the life of the world.[80]

Theologian Gregory Baum once noted that "only if religion becomes uncreative, repetitive, tied to the past, unable to bring forth new responses in the present, does it die in the hearts of men."[81] Vatican II's teaching on the potential vitality of the local church is an example of the council's attempt to keep religion and faith alive in the hearts of the faithful.

We look now to one final dimension of Vatican II's understanding of the church, that it is a pilgrim people of God on a journey through history, moving toward its final destiny: God.

The Church Is a Reality in the Making

The period between Vatican I and Vatican II was a time of significant growth and development in the field of ecclesiology. Many changes occurred. And, as we saw earlier, this notion of "change" proved very disturbing to those who subscribed to the classicist worldview. For them, change implied mistake. Of course, if you are of the mind that your church can be identified with the one true church of Christ, the kingdom of God on earth, and that your church possesses an absolute certitude about all matters pertaining to the faith, then such an attitude might be quite understandable. This, of course, was not the view taken by the "new theologians." They knew that there were some elements of the faith that belonged to the very essence of the faith and would endure always. They also knew that there were other elements that could change—in fact, must change—as the church moved through history. When John Henry Newman wrote his well-known *Essay on the Development of Christian Doctrine* in 1845, his goal was "not to explain *how* doctrine develops but *that* doctrine develops."[82] In fact, it was the thinking found in this essay that finally led Newman to convert to Catholicism. His examination of the history of Christianity demonstrated that all things do develop and change over time, even the church. Newman became convinced that the church was capable of infinite growth.[83] Newman's position finds a home in *Lumen Gentium*. In the very first article, we find a remarkable statement: "The church desires now to *unfold more fully* to the faithful of the church and to the whole world its own inner nature."[84] This statement is indeed remarkable given the mindset toward "change" in the decades before the council.

This notion of "unfolding" can be traced back to many of the "new theologians," especially those associated with the Tübingen School. Johann Sebastian von Drey had insisted that "it is characteristic of Christian doctrine to unfold itself ever more clearly."[85]

One could almost believe that von Drey had written the following comment from *Lumen Gentium:*

> The Word of God is compared to a seed which is sown in a field; those who hear the Word with faith and become part of the little flock of Christ, have received the Kingdom in itself. Then, by its own power, the seed sprouts and grows until harvest time.[86]

This "unfolding" is inherent in the divine plan. We need not fear it. Karl Rahner believed that God as "absolute future" was the key to the church's future. According to Rahner, "Until the *eschaton*...the church (would continue) to exist in history and remain subject to the conditions of history (which would involve) the unpredictability of history and the need to move forward."[87]

This last quote contains two very important notions: that of history and that of the *eschaton*. Regarding history, church historian John O'Malley contends that with their acceptance of historical consciousness, the worldview that recognizes that all expressions of theological truth are conditioned by their moment in history, the council fathers came to agree that changes would be required to meet the needs of the times.[88] Clearly, what we find in *Lumen Gentium* is a dynamic understanding of church. By virtue of the incarnation, the church entered into human history (a position that was central to the theology of M.-D. Chenu)...it is affected by history and it moves toward a final destination. This appreciation for human history and its connection to the faith would prove to be decisive for the direction taken by the council,[89] as seen in this statement from *Lumen Gentium:*

> God gathered together as one all who in faith look upon Jesus as the author of salvation and the source of unity and peace, and established them as the church that for each and all it may be the visible sacrament of this saving unity. While it transcends all limits of time and confines of race, the church is destined to extend to all regions of the earth and so *enters the history of mankind.*[90]

One can easily discern the influence of Yves Congar here. In 1934, he had written:

> To every growth of humanity, to every bit of progress…there should correspond a growth in the church…an incarnation of grace, a humanization of God! That is the church….The church is not…a separate entity remaining untouched among the evolving realities of the world….The church…is Christ dwelling in the world and saving it by our faith.[91]

The other important notion contained in the earlier reference from Rahner involves the *eschaton*. Eschatology is that branch of theology that deals with issues relating to the "end time." It examines the kingdom of God as understood in the Old Testament's preparation for this kingdom (for example, the messianic hopes) and in the teaching of Jesus and the early church. It points to the fact that our present existence is future directed.[92] As such, it expresses an openness to a world in the making. Vatican II moved away from a rigid concept of orthodoxy, which had become separated from its life-giving sources—scripture and tradition. Hence, our grasp of theological truths needs to be influenced by the council's acknowledgment of the church as an eschatological reality. This is a reality in process, a promise to be fulfilled and not an end in itself.[93]

The eschatological dimension of the church carries profound implications for the church's self-understanding. For one thing, the church can no longer identify herself with the kingdom, an idea that prevailed in pre–Vatican II ecclesiology. Rather, she is a sign pointing to the future kingdom promised us by God. Also, the church cannot be viewed as an end in itself. Instead, she serves as an instrument of the Spirit of Christ. "Its task is to be such an instrument—if always a human, and therefore a sin-burdened instrument for the Word of God and the Spirit of God." And because she is "sin-burdened," it is never permitted to divinize the church itself or any of its institutional components.[94] These implications are laid out clearly in *Lumen Gentium*:

The church...will attain its full perfection only in the glory of heaven....At that time the human race...will be perfectly reestablished in Christ....Already the final age of the world has come upon us and the renovation of the world is irrevocably decreed and is already anticipated in some kind of real way; for the church already on this earth is signed with a sanctity which is real although imperfect. However, until there shall be new heavens and a new earth in which justice dwells, the Pilgrim Church in her sacraments and institutions, which pertain to this present time, has the appearance of this world which is passing and she herself dwells among creatures who groan and travail in pain until now and await the revelation of the sons of God.[95]

This quote from *Lumen Gentium* reveals two other very significant developments in the church's self-understanding: (1) Because the church is an eschatological reality, the faithful are referred to as a "pilgrim people" of God. They are on their way to the kingdom, to the fullness of truth who is God. (2) The holiness enjoyed by the faithful is an imperfect holiness. And, as with previously discussed dimensions of *Lumen Gentium*'s ecclesiology, these elements also carry profound theological implications.

The idea of the church as a pilgrim people of God on a journey through history certainly supports those theologians who for years had been calling for structural changes in the church. This concept can be considered something of a mandate for ongoing reform and renewal. Yves Congar had maintained that genuine reform would be recognized by an openness to adapt the structures of church life to new situations, to refuse to let any stage in the life of the church be considered definitive, claiming that along the journey the ecclesiastical apparatus must never be permitted to obscure God's grace.[96] Congar knew that those who had accepted the legitimacy of historical studies and historical thinking were better prepared for what would occur at the council. He also knew that there would be others who would be disturbed because they possessed "a monolithic, monarchic, and wholly divinized view of the church,"[97] a perception that Congar considered a fallacy. Congar recognized that the gospel offered an ideal that the human church could never fully achieve. Therefore, there is an ongoing need to look critically at historical forms of the church in an effort to bring the church ever closer to the ideal.[98] And, in the mind of Karl Rahner, to suggest that the customs and discipline of the church of the West could be considered the norm for the entire church was a heresy.[99] Along these lines, John Henry Newman had been concerned that the church was making religion into a "system," running the risk of the earthly reality of church becoming an object of our devotion instead of God.[100]

One consequence of being a pilgrim people moving toward the *eschaton* is that our holiness is imperfect. *Lumen Gentium* makes this clear in its comparison of the church with the Incarnate Word. It points to the presence of both the human and the divine in each. However, the document makes a very important distinction between the two, as seen in a section of *Lumen Gentium* discussed previously. It speaks of Christ, who is holy, innocent, and undefiled. But it goes on to add, "The church, embracing in its bosom sinners, at the same time holy and always in need of being purified, always follows the way of penance and renewal."[101] Perhaps Karl Rahner captures the meaning of our "imperfect holiness" best. It was mentioned earlier that his belief in the church as the sacrament of salvation did not lead him to an idealized vision of church. Rahner was very much aware of the weaknesses present in the church:

> We are always playing the incomplete symphony of the glory of God and it is always only a dress rehearsal. But all the hardship, the always incomplete reform is not in vain, not senseless. It is simply the task of servants who sow in tears, so that God may harvest....[102]

All of this talk about imperfect holiness and the need for ongoing purification and reform might lead one to feel some pessimism about the church, who, "like a stranger in a foreign land, presses forward amid the persecutions of the world."[103] But our theologians have a remedy for such thinking: the gift of the Holy Spirit.

In 1825, Johann Adam Mohler wrote, "The church is the external, visible form of a holy, living power of love, which the Holy Spirit imparts."[104] Karl Rahner claimed that the Spirit was responsible for "the development and unfolding of the original treasure of faith."[105] And, according to M.-D. Chenu, "Through the mediation of the Holy Spirit, the eschatological end time is active as a dimension of the present."[106] The important role of the Holy Spirit was not lost on the council fathers either. *Lumen Gentium* takes seriously the promises of the risen Christ that he would send his Spirit, as well as the insights of our theologians in this regard:

> When the work which the Father gave the Son to do on earth was accomplished, the Holy Spirit was sent on the day of Pentecost in order that He might continually sanctify the church....The Spirit dwells in the church and in the hearts of the faithful....Uninterruptedly, He renews it and leads it to perfect union [with Christ].

Again, further on in the document:

> Moving forward through trial and tribulation, the church is strengthened by the power of God's grace...and, moved by the Holy Spirit, may never cease to renew herself, until through the cross she arrives at the light which knows no setting.[107]

When a central role is given to the Holy Spirit, "the church is never a *fait accompli*....It is always an eschatological reality, a people-to-be, constituted in communion...on its pilgrim way to the triune God."[108]

At the 2004 meeting of the Catholic Theological Society of America, Joseph Komonchak offered the following, very appropriate reflection regarding Yves Congar's belief in the Holy Spirit: "Congar compared the Holy Spirit to an aquifer, a source of fresh water lying beneath the ground until here or there...from it bubbles up a spring to water the earth again and make it fruitful in new places."[109] It is this belief that gives hope and confidence to the pilgrim people of God on their journey to their ultimate destiny—union with their God.

Conclusion

"Whenever it abandons a system of thought, humanity imagines it has lost God."[110] It seems fitting to use this quote from Henri de Lubac as we put together some concluding thoughts on this chapter, which looked at how the church's self-understanding changed between Vatican I and Vatican II. At Vatican II, the council fathers did abandon a system of thought: neoscholasticism. Led by the insights of those theologians who for years had been calling for a new language to speak about the faith, the council fathers rediscovered in the New Testament a language that gives life. In their retrieval of the ecclesial concepts and images from the early church—mystery, pilgrim people of God, importance of the local church, and the reality of the *eschaton* with its profound theological implications—they brought about a major change in the way the church looked at herself. No longer was the church to be viewed as a pyramid, a hierarchical model in which holiness was determined by one's placement on the pyramid. Vatican II offered another way of being church: the *communio* model, where one's holiness is determined by one's response to the graces given by God. We abandoned a *juridical* vision and opted for a *theological* vision. *Lumen Gentium* was the voice for this new vision.

This Dogmatic Constitution on the Church was overwhelmingly approved on November 21, 1964. The vote was 2,151 to 5, making *Lumen Gentium* the "Magna Carta for any subsequent reflection on the church in the Roman Catholic tradition."[111] The ecclesiology of the preconciliar church had lost touch with its roots in the New Testament. It was highly authoritarian, legalistic, and clericalistic. It possessed a "state of siege" mentality and was fearful and suspicious of the world with which it shared a history. But a sufficient number of council fathers sought to bring about a change:

> a change in this closed, ghetto-like, authoritarian style....(They) wanted to open the church to what was valid and helpful (in the modern world), much of which was a retrieval of its own deepest traditions....(They) did not want to turn the church into a democracy...but they did want to redefine how...authority was to function,

namely, with a respect for conscience that transformed church members, especially the laity, from "subjects" to participants....(They) insisted the church, like all good teachers, needed to learn as it taught.[112]

Only those who had lived through this remarkable transition from a hierarchical church to an ecclesiology of communion can remember and perhaps appreciate the challenges this change would offer the church. As de Lubac noted, "Whenever it abandons a system of thought, humanity imagines it has lost God." No doubt, there were those who thought they had lost God. The changes proposed by *Lumen Gentium* alone would be difficult for most of the faithful to comprehend. After all, their church had not changed for close to four hundred years. Nor did these members have a sufficient theological education to prepare them for an event of this magnitude in the life of the church. The unchangeable cannot change...but it did. And *Lumen Gentium* was the messenger of this fact. However...we did not lose God.

In our discussions of the various theologians who prepared the way for Vatican II, one thing becomes very clear: they were convinced that the Holy Spirit was alive and well and active in the church. They took seriously the words from John's Gospel: "When the Spirit of truth comes, he will guide you into all the truth...and he will declare to you the things that are to come."[113] Their confidence was grounded in a profound theological concept known as indefectibility. This principle is rooted in the instructions given to the disciples in Matthew's Gospel: "Go therefore and make disciples of all nations, baptizing them in the name of the Father, and of the Son, and of the Holy Spirit, and teaching them to obey everything that I have commanded you. And, remember, I am with you always, to the end of the age."[114] This quote is an assurance from the risen Christ that sin will never so dominate the church that it could be totally unfaithful to God's truth, a truth that unfolds ever more fully through history. No human weakness, no failure, no human system of thought can fully obscure God's grace. In essence, the church is a mystery in that it includes both human and divine elements. Because of the human component, the church is not perfect, nor will it ever be. The promise of the risen Christ to be faithful to his church assures us that, despite our sinfulness, despite our imperfect attempts to articulate revelation in human words and systems of thought, error will not have the final word, even though partial errors and human failures are always possible. Vatican II gave support to the indefectibility principle in *Gaudium et Spes*:

> Although by the power of the Holy Spirit the church will remain the faithful spouse of her Lord and will never cease to be the sign of salvation on earth, still she is very aware that among her members, both clerical and lay, some have been unfaithful to the Spirit of God through the course of the centuries....It does not escape the church how great a distance lies between the message she offers and the human failings of those to whom the Gospel is entrusted....Led by the Holy Spirit, Mother Church unceasingly exhorts her sons to purify and renew themselves so that the sign of Christ can shine more brightly....[115]

"Led by the Holy Spirit..." is the operative concept here. Systems of thought, theological articulations of the faith, and worldviews are simply the vehicles through which we attempt to bring God to birth again in each new generation. But these vehicles are historical realities. They can change, grow, and develop. There is, however, one constant: the gift of the Holy Spirit. This is what our theologians came to understand and this is what sustained them during the darker moments of their personal theological journeys. When Yves Congar learned of John XXIII's decision to convene a church council, he remarked, "This could make sense only in faith. If it has been without reflection...then what a catastrophe! Or, it is the work of the Holy Spirit, in which case everything is possible."[116] For Congar and for the other theologians we have encountered in these pages, the Holy Spirit was indeed the interior principle in the life of the church, the principle by which the incarnation of Christ continues.[117]

So...we have not lost God. The God who is our origin, our sustenance, and our destiny is very much with us in our struggle to be the pilgrim people of God. The words of Blaise Pascal come to mind: "It is a happy time for the church when she is sustained by nothing other than God."[118] The Spirit of God is indeed with us on our journey. When we look back at the "bumpy road" of theology between Vatican I and Vatican II, the presence of the Holy Spirit cannot be denied. We moved from a mindset of condemnation to one of dialogue, from a ghetto-like existence, isolated from the world to an acknowledgment of the worth of that world and a desire to engage that world, from a fortress-like mentality, defensive against potential threats from the outside world to a recognition that the church is a communion and is always dependent on God's grace. It is a church that wants to be "seen as a reminder, as the guardian of unchanging values…as a lamp placed on a lampstand, as the spring of living water at which we all can drink."[119] And the journey has proved the wisdom of these words from Cardinal Suenens: "The history of Christianity is for us a school of humility. This same history is also a school of hope."[120]

EPILOGUE

The presence of great thinkers is something that cannot
be planned: it happens; it surprises us; it is experienced as
a special gift of God.[1]

The "Prophets"

These words of theologian Gregory Baum serve as a fitting
way to begin to offer some closing thoughts about our journey from
Vatican I to Vatican II, a journey made all the more memorable by
the presence of those prophets among us. Indeed, they were a special gift of God to the church. Baum offered this tribute during an
interview he gave talking about his experience at the Second Vatican
Council. A similar recollection is provided by theologian Ladislas
Orsy, SJ. He tells how the "new theologians" who had been disciplined by the official church in the years leading up to Vatican II
were ultimately vindicated. Once in Rome for the council, these
same theologians were being invited to give seminars to the bishops
and even helping to draft the conciliar documents. As Orsy tells it,
"The once-exiled experts were offering new wine to the shepherds,
and the shepherds liked it."[2]

I came across the following quote recently that brought these
theologians to mind:

But none of the ransomed ever knew
How deep were the waters crossed.[3]

When I was finally able to locate the source of the quote, I found
that it was a poem about the good shepherd who left his ninety-nine

sheep to search for the one who had wandered away. But those two lines by themselves could be applied to those theologians who labored for years to change theology and to prepare the ground for the Second Vatican Council. Their influence on the documents of Vatican II is undeniable. Yet, as we have seen, their ultimate vindication at the council came with a price. Some of them lived long enough to witness the profound impact they had on the church. Others did not. I wonder if any of us, whose lives were changed by these theologians, could ever imagine "how deep were the waters crossed." In December 1963, there was a gathering in Strasbourg to honor Yves Congar. One of the guests, Prof. Oscar Cullmann, offered the following tribute to Congar—but, in truth, it could have been said about all the theologians we have encountered on this journey:

> In talking about man's role in the context of salvation history, there is no danger of exaggerating the human elements in it—for it is understood that, in this history, there are only instruments of Christ, and we know that what we owe to you we owe to an Other who has made use of you.[4]

The Documents of Vatican II

In a book about Catholic identity after the council, Frans Jozef van Beeck makes an important observation. He claims that the council brought about a truly significant rearrangement of the basic themes of the Catholic faith.[5] In this book, we have not studied all the "themes" that were rearranged at the council. Nor have we examined all the documents. But, in those that we have chosen to discuss, van Beeck's claim has been evidenced.

Here, we note some examples. For one thing, we found a renewed appreciation for the role of history. The church, once viewed as timeless and immutable, is now portrayed as dynamic and developing. In their acceptance of the historically conscious worldview, the council fathers acknowledged the impact of history on all living organisms—a realization that in history God's eternal plan manifests itself in time.

We also discovered that a previous juridical vision of church (hierarchical model) was replaced by a theological vision (*communio* model). And, in this *communio* model, particularly in *Lumen Gentium* and *Apostolicam Actuositatem*, we found a new understanding of the layperson in the church. The layperson is now accorded the full dignity he or she received at baptism. No longer mere "helpers of the hierarchy," laymen and women have a distinctive mission of their own in the church. And, in the council's call for universal holiness, we came to see that one's "state of grace" is not contingent on one's vocation. All baptized members are called to be holy.

In *Gaudium et Spes*, the law of incarnation found a home in the church once again. The incarnation reveals that the presence and transforming power of the divine can be manifest in visible, created realities. Therefore, all things—even the world that we had kept at a distance for so many years—can be an instrument of grace. As we learned from Karl Rahner, "For the believer, the history of the world is the history of grace."[6]

A comparison of the documents from Vatican II with those of the First Vatican Council indicates another significant "rearrangement": the bishops at Vatican II opted for a language that gives life. They found this language in the Bible with its rich concepts of mystery, covenant, pilgrim people of God. In choosing this—and rejecting the neoscholastic language of preconciliar documents—the council fathers were acknowledging another important development in the church: the people of God had reached a point in their journey where "understanding" the faith (heart knowledge) was equally important as "knowing" the faith (head knowledge). And, as we tried to show in the preceding chapters, each new "rearrangement" of the understanding of the faith carried with it profound implications for the lived experience of the faith.

One more thing should be noted regarding the Vatican II documents. Perhaps Yves Congar expresses the point best:

> The danger is that one will not *seek* anymore, but will simply exploit the inexhaustible warehouse of Vatican II.…It would be a betrayal of the *aggiornamento* if we thought it could be fixed once and for all in the texts of Vatican II.[7]

We find overwhelming agreement in this regard, both from those who participated in the council and those who have written about it.[8] One council observer, Dr. Donal Kerr, made a particularly insightful comment after the council: "Though we did not realize it then, we were present at perhaps the greatest and most comprehensive theological discourse the Christian world has seen."[9] Insightful words, indeed.

The Holy Spirit

Early on in the introduction to this book, I wrote that I wanted to tell the story of the journey between the two Vatican Councils through the lens of the Holy Spirit. One simply cannot make sense of this journey unless the Holy Spirit is acknowledged as the guiding principle and the source of life in the church. As Congar remarked when he heard that a new council was being convened by Pope John XXIII, if "it is the work of the Holy Spirit, then everything is possible."[10]

Ever since Pope Pius XII issued his encyclical *Divino Afflante Spiritu*, Catholic biblical scholars have opened our eyes to deeper and richer insights in the Bible. They came to see that theological truth was not contingent on mere historical accuracy. The scriptures bring us the truth we need for our salvation. So, when we read that the Spirit of Christ will be sent to teach us all things,[11] we know those words mean something. Do we understand them as a promise to be kept or as a spiritual sentiment? They are meant to be taken as a promise of the risen Christ to be faithful to his church: "But when he comes, the Spirit of truth, he will guide you to all truth."[12]

The Future

At the conclusion of the Second Vatican Council, Yves Congar wrote, "The future is open for an advance to new stages. The Lord who has begun this great work will know how to complete it."[13] Four decades have passed since the council ended, and, of course, God continues to "complete" the great work begun there. So many developments have occurred since the council ended, but "that story" must be told by someone else. It was my task to look at the journey from Pius IX at Vatican I to John XXIII at Vatican II and to discover the contributions of those remarkable theologians who planted seeds that would come to fruition at Vatican II. Because of the specific focus taken in this book, we did not cover all of the significant themes taken up at the council. Another story for another book, perhaps. For now, it seems clear that—in agreement with Karl Rahner—"the Council was the beginning of the beginning."[14]

Pope John XXIII hoped and prayed that the Second Vatican Council would be a new Pentecost, when the Holy Spirit would again bring new life to the church. It is fair to say that John's prayer was indeed answered. His absolute trust in the Spirit of God is perhaps his greatest legacy. This belief in the Holy Spirit was shared by another great leader of Vatican II, Leon Joseph Cardinal Suenens. When asked once why he was a man of hope, he said because he believed in the Holy Spirit. In a prayer written by Suenens to further explain his trust in the Spirit, he wrote:

> I believe in the surprises of the Holy Spirit.
> John XXIII came as a surprise, and the council, too.
> They were the last things we expected.
> Who would dare to say that the love and imagination
>   of God were exhausted.
> To hope is a duty, not a luxury.[15]

The modern church, now into the third millennium, can offer no greater tribute to the memory of Pope John XXIII, to the great theologians who served the church so well and to the achievements of the Second Vatican Council than to be for the world a witness of hope.

NOTES

Introduction

1. Joseph Komonchak, "Vatican Council as Ecumenical Council: Yves Congar's Vision Realized," *Commonweal* 129:20 (November 22, 2002), 12. Available at http://www.jknirp.com/congar4.htm.

2. Bishop Frank Markus Fernando, "Interview," in *Voices from the Council*, eds. Michael R. Prendergast and M. D. Ridge (Portland, OR: Pastoral Press, 2004), 19.

3. John E. Benson, "The History of the Historical Critical Method in the Church: A Survey," *Dialog* 12 (1973), 94–103, at 95.

4. Dianne Bergant, CSA, "Sacred Scripture: Light for Our Path," *Vatican II Today* (June 2004). Available at http://www.AmericanCatholic.org/Newsletter/VAT/aq0604.asp.

5. Bergant, "Sacred Scripture," 1.

6. Pope Pius XII, *Divino Afflante Spiritu*, in The Papal Encyclicals 1939–1958, ed. Claudia Carlen, IHM (Raleigh, NC: Pierian Press, 1990), 65–79.

7. Brendan Byrne, SJ, "Scripture and Vatican II: A Very Incomplete Journey," *Compass* 38 (Winter 2003). Available at http://www.compassreview.org/winter03/2.html.

8. 1 Corinthians 7:25, 32.

9. Leonard Swidler, *Toward a Catholic Constitution* (New York: Crossroad Publishing Company, 1966), 4, 5.

Chapter 1: Theology in Transition

1. Reynold Borzaga, *In Pursuit of Religion: A Framework for Understanding Today's Theology* (Palm Springs, FL: Sunday Publications, 1977), 19.

2. Borzaga, *In Pursuit of Religion*, 21.

3. Pope John XXIII, "Opening Address of the Second Vatican Council," October 11, 1962.

4. Matthew 5:48.

5. Borzaga, *In Pursuit of Religion*, 63.

6. *Gaudium et Spes* in *The Documents of Vatican II*, 11 July 2004, 1. Hereafter referred to as GS. Available online at http://www.vatican.va/archive/hist_councils/ii_vatican_council/documents/vat-ii_const_19651207_gaudium-et-spes_en.html.

7. Monica Hellwig, "Foundations for Theology," in *Faithful Witness*, eds. Leo J. O'Donovan and T. Howland Sanks (New York: Crossroad Publishing Company, 1989), 1–13, at 11.

8. Aidan Nichols, OP, *The Shape of Catholic Theology* (Collegeville, MN: Liturgical Press, 1991), 12–35; quotes at 27, 29, and 31.

9. Timothy McCarthy, *The Catholic Tradition: Before and after Vatican II 1878–1993* (Chicago: Loyola University Press, 1994), 56.

10. McCarthy, *Catholic Tradition*, 57.

11. Yves Congar, OP, *Report from Rome: First Session*, trans. A. Manson (London: Geoffrey Chapman Ltd., 1963), 92.

12. Joseph Komonchak, "Vatican II as Ecumenical Council: Yves Congar's Vision Realized," *Commonweal* 129:20 (November 22, 2002), 12. Available at http://www.jknirp.com/congar4.htm.

13. Dennis Doyle, "Different Schools of Reform Led to Vatican II," address given at the University of Dayton, October 31, 1997.

14. Quoted in James Bacik, *Contemporary Theologians* (Chicago: Thomas More Press, 1989), 48, from Yves Congar's *Dialogue between Christians* (Westminster, MD: Newman Press, 1966), 34.

15. Robert Nugent, SDS, "Yves Congar: Apostle of Patience," *Australian EJournal of Theology*, no. 4 (February 2005). Available at http://dlibrary.acu.edu.au/research/theology/ejournal/aejt_4/nugent.htm.

16. Bacik, *Contemporary Theologians*, 11–16.

17. Michael Fahey, SJ, "Church," in *Systematic Theology: Roman Catholic Perspectives*, Vol. II, eds. Francis Schüssler Fiorenza and John P. Galvin (Minneapolis: Fortress Press, 1991), 1–74, at 5.

18. Matthew 13:57.

19. Vatican Council I, *Dogmatic Constitution on the Church*, in Norman Tanner, SJ, ed., Decrees of the Ecumenical Councils, 2; Trent-Vatican II (Lanham, MD: Sheed & Ward, 1990), 811–16.

20. Joseph Komonchak, "Return from Exile: Catholic Theology in the 1930s," in *The Twentieth Century: A Theological Overview*, ed. Gregory Baum (Maryknoll, NY: Orbis Books, 1999), 35–48, at 40.

21. Joseph Komonchak, "Theology and Culture at Mid-Century: The Example of Henri de Lubac," *Theological Studies* 51:4 (December 1990), 579–610, at 580.

22. Komonchak, "Return from Exile," 44.

23. Paul-Emile Cardinal Leger, "Introduction," in *Theology of Renewal*, Vol. I, ed. L. K. Schook, CSB (Montreal: Palm Publishers, 1968), 19–33, at 20.

24. Leger, "Introduction," 22. See Yves Congar, *Vraie et Fausse Reforme dans l'Eglise* (Paris: Editions du Cerf, 1950), 179.

25. James M. Connolly, *The Voices of France* (New York: Macmillan Company, 1961), 82.

26. James C. Livingston, *Modern Christian Thought: From the Enlightenment to Vatican II*, Vol. I (New Jersey: Prentice-Hall, 1971), 188.

27. Livingston, *Modern Christian Thought*, 191.

28. Livingston, *Modern Christian Thought*, 193.

29. Livingston, *Modern Christian Thought*, 197.

30. Michael J. Himes, "The Development of Ecclesiology: Modernity to the Twentieth Century," in *Gift of the Church*, ed. Peter C. Phan (Collegeville, MN: Liturgical Press, 2000), 45–67, at 58.

31. Himes, "Development of Ecclesiology," 59.

32. Samuel D. Femiano, *Infallibility of the Laity: The Legacy of Newman* (New York: Herder & Herder, 1967).

33. Femiano, *Infallibility of the Laity*, xii.

34. Werner Becker, "Newman's Influence in Germany," in *The Rediscovery of Newman: An Oxford Symposium*, eds. John Coulson and A. M. Allchin (London: Sheed & Ward, 1967), 174–189, at 189.

35. Pope Paul VI, *L'Osservatore Romano* (Italian language ed.), April 7–8, 1975, 1.

36. Ian T. Ker, "Newman and the Postconciliar Church," in *Newman Today*, 1988 Proceedings of the Wethersfield Institute, Vol. 1, ed. Stanley L. Jaki (San Francisco: Ignatius Press, 1989), 121–41, at 121.

37. Avery Dulles, *Newman* (London and New York: Continuum, 2002), 151.

38. Dulles, *Newman*, 158.

39. T. M. Schoof, *A Survey of Catholic Theology, 1800–1970*, trans. N. D. Smith (Glen Rock, NJ: Paulist Newman Press, 1970). There are astonishing parallels between Newman's ideas and those of the Catholic theologians of Tübingen, although specialists in the field have, with some surprise, come to the conclusion that it is only in a very remote sense that any connection can be made between Newman, who began to look in very much the same direction as the Tübingen School at least twenty-five years after von Drey.

40. Livingston, *Modern Christian Thought*, 202.

41. John Henry Newman, *An Essay on the Development of Doctrine, 1878* (Notre Dame, IN: University of Notre Dame Press, 1989), 30.

42. Livingston, *Modern Christian Thought*, 190–91.

43. Dulles, *Newman*, 7.

44. Newman, *Essay on Development*, 39.

45. Newman, *Essay on Development*, 40.

46. Dulles, *Newman*, 12.

47. Louis Bouyer, "The Permanent Relevance of Newman," in *Newman Today*, ed. Jaki, 165–74, at 165.

48. Livingston, *Modern Christian Thought*, 189.

49. See John R. Quinn, *The Reform of the Papacy* (New York: Crossroad Publishing Company, 1999), 77: "This position was present in Vatican I and is called the 'maximalist' interpretation of papal primacy. While this position was not the teaching of Vatican I or of its definition of primacy, it was in the air, so to speak, and has continued from that time to this in segments of the Roman Curia and elsewhere in the church." See also Yves Congar, *Eglise et Papaute* (Paris: Editions du Cerf, 1994), 279.

50. John Henry Newman, *Letters and Diaries*, Vol. XXV, 278, 310. See *The Letters and Diaries of John Henry Newman*, ed. with notes and intro. Ian Ker and Thomas Gornall (Oxford: Clarendon Press, 1979).

51. John Henry Newman, *Letters and Diaries*, Vol. XIX, 140.

52. John Henry Newman, *Letters on the Present Position of Catholics in England* (New York: America Press, 1942), 300.

53. Paul Misner, "Romano Guardini," in *New Catholic Encyclopedia*, Vol. 6 (Detroit, MI: Thomas/Gale; Washington, DC: Catholic University of America, 2003), 550.

54. John 1:1.

55. Robert A. Krieg, CSC, *Romano Guardini: A Precursor of Vatican II* (Notre Dame, IN: University of Notre Dame Press, 1997), 41.

56. Krieg, *Romano Guardini*, 176.

57. Krieg, *Romano Guardini*, 168.

58. Krieg, *Romano Guardini*, 88.

59. Karl-Heinz Weger, *Karl Rahner: An Introduction to His Theology* (New York: Crossroad/Seabury Press, 1980), 2ff.

60. Weger, *Karl Rahner*, 5.

61. Karl Rahner, SJ, *Foundations of Christian Faith: An Introduction to the Idea of Christianity*, trans. William V. Dych (New York: Crossroad/Seabury Press, 1982), 449.

62. Geoffrey B. Kelly, ed., *Karl Rahner: Theologian of the Graced Search for Meaning* (Minneapolis: Fortress Press, 1992), 44.

63. Weger, *Karl Rahner*, 55.

64. Thomas O'Meara, OP, "A History of Grace," in *A World of Grace*, ed. Leo J. O'Donovan (New York: Crossroad, 1981), 76–91, at 77.

65. Kelly, *Karl Rahner*, 49.

66. Weger, *Karl Rahner*, 169.

67. Walter Kasper, *Jesus the Christ* (London and New York: Paulist Press, 1976), 121.

68. Leo J. O'Donovan, "In Memoriam: Karl Rahner, SJ, 1904–1984," *Journal of the American Academy of Religion* 53:1 (March 1985), 129–131, at 130.

Chapter 2: The Church Looks at the World

1. John 14:26.

2. See Thomas Bokenkotter, *A Concise History of the Catholic Church*, rev. and exp. ed. (New York: Doubleday, 1990), 63: "Jerome repeatedly exalts virginity in these treatises as the only appropriate state in life for the committed Christian."

3. *Gaudium et Spes* in *The Documents of Vatican II*, 11 July 2004, 44. Hereafter referred to as GS. Available online at http://www.vatican.va/archive/hist_councils/ii_vatican_council/documents/vat-ii_const_19651207_gaudium-et-spes_en.html.

4. GS 2.

5. GS 37.

6. Yves Congar, OP, "Moving toward a Pilgrim Church," in *Vatican II Revisited by Those Who Were There*, ed. Dom Alberic Stacpoole, OSB (Minneapolis: Winston Press, 1986), 129–52, at 144.

7. "How Vatican II Turned the Church toward the World," *Time*, December 17, 1965, pp. 24–25.

8. "How Vatican II," p. 24.

9. "How Vatican II," p. 25.

10. GS 2.

11. GS 3.

12. Robert A. Krieg, CSC, "A Precursor's Life and Work," in *Romano Guardini: Proclaiming the Sacred in a Modern World*, ed. Robert A. Krieg, CSC (Chicago: Liturgy Training Publications, 1995), 15–29, at 26.

13. Yves Congar, OP, "Theology's Tasks after Vatican II," in *Theology of Renewal*, Vol. I, ed. L. K. Shook, CSB (Montreal: Palm Publishers, 1968), 47–65, at 57, 59.

14. Patrick Granfield, *Theologians at Work* (New York: Macmillan Company, 1967), xviii, 246.

15. Christophe Potworowski, *Contemplation and Incarnation: The Theology of Marie-Dominique Chenu* (Montreal, Quebec, Canada: McGill-Queen's University Press, 2001), xiv–xv.

16. Potworowski, *Contemplation*, 85.

17. GS 39.

18. Pope John XXIII, *Pacem in Terris*, in *The Papal Encyclicals 1958–1981*, ed. Claudia Carlen, IHM (Raleigh, NC: Pierian Press, 1990), 107–29.

19. Potworowski, *Contemplation*, 174.

20. Matthew 5:48.

21. Karl-Heinz Weger, *Karl Rahner: An Introduction to His Theology* (New York: Crossroad/Seabury Press, 1980), 55.

22. John Coulson and A. M. Allchin, eds., *The Rediscovery of Newman: An Oxford Symposium* (London: SPCK, 1967), xviii.

23. Robert A. Krieg, CSC, *Romano Guardini: A Precursor of Vatican II* (Notre Dame, IN: University of Notre Dame Press, 1997), 175.

24. Edward Quinn, "Renewal of Theology," *Downside Review* 74 (October 1956), 289–301, at 294.

25. Weger, *Karl Rahner*, 55.

26. John P. Galvin, "The Invitation of Grace," in *A World of Grace*, ed. Leo J. O'Donovan (New York: Crossroad, 1981), 64–75, at 66.

27. GS 19.

28. GS 14.

29. See Dermot A. Lane, *Experience, God and Theology* (New York: Paulist Press, 1981), 16: "If we did not already know God implicitly in our experiences we could not even begin to raise the question of God. When we do find God explicitly in our experiences we are recognizing what was there all along....The central point here is that the presence of God in the world, communicated through the religious dimension of human experience, is neither a presence directly available only to a privileged few nor a presence mediated simply through logical deduction to the learned. Instead the reality of God in the world is a presence that is accessible to all."

30. GS 38.

31. GS 10.

32. Weger, *Karl Rahner,* 164.

33. GS 22.

34. Romano Guardini, *Das Wesen des Christentums* (Wurzburg: Echter, 1938), 5 and 68. This text first appeared in 1929.

35. GS 44.

36. GS 44.

37. GS 53.

38. GS 53.

39. GS 58.

40. GS 31.

41. Daniel O'Hanlon, "Concluding Reflections," in *Current Trends in Theology*, eds. Donald Wolf, SJ, and James Schall, SJ (Garden City, NY: Doubleday and Company, 1965), 271–77, at 273.

42. Ian T. Ker, "Newman and the Postconciliar Church," in *Newman Today*, Vol. 1, 1988 Proceedings of the Wethersfield Institute, ed. Stanley L. Jaki (San Francisco: Ignatius Press, 1989), 121–41, at 126, from Newman's *Letters and Diaries*, Vol. XX, 477.

43. Jean-Pierre Jossua, OP, *Yves Congar: Theology in the Service of God's People* (Chicago: Priory Press, 1968), 52.

44. Michael Himes, "The Development of Ecclesiology: Modernity to the Twentieth Century," in *The Gift of the Church*, ed. Peter C. Phan (Collegeville, MN: Liturgical Press, 2000), 45–67, at 56.

45. William V. Dych, "Theology in a New Key," in *A World of Grace*, ed. Leo J. O'Donovan (New York: Crossroad, 1981), 1–16, at 2.

46. Pope John XXIII, "Opening Address of the Second Vatican Council," October 11, 1962.

47. GS 2.

48. Walter Kasper, *The Methods of Dogmatic Theology*, trans. John Drury (New York: Paulist Press, 1969), 64.

49. Avery Dulles, SJ, *Newman* (London and New York: Continuum, 2002), 74.

50. John Henry Newman, *Essay on the Development of Doctrine* (London: Pickering, 1878).

51. Potworowski, *Contemplation*, 195.

52. Jossua, *Yves Congar*, 110.

53. Jossua, *Yves Congar*, 111.

54. Michael Buckley, "Within the Holy Mystery," in *A World of Grace*, ed. Leo J. O'Donovan (New York: Crossroad, 1981), 31–49, at 40.

55. Pope John XXIII, "Opening Address."

56. GS 62.

57. GS 62.

58. GS 5.

59. GS 91.

60. Quoted in Timothy O'Connell, "Vatican II: Setting, Themes, Future Agenda," in *Vatican II and Its Documents: An American Appraisal*, ed. Timothy O'Connell (Wilmington, DE: Michael Glazier, 1986), 237–55, at 244, from John O'Malley, SJ, "Reform, Historical Consciousness and Vatican II's *Aggiornamento*," Theological Studies 32 (1971), 573–601.

61. Jossua, *Yves Congar*, 115.

62. Jossua, *Yves Congar*, 33.

63. "How Vatican II," p. 25.

Chapter 3: The Church Looks at the Laity

1. Charles Stephen Dessain, *John Henry Newman* (London: Thomas Nelson & Sons, 1966), 117.

2. Robert A. Burns, OP, *Roman Catholicism after Vatican II* (Washington, DC: Georgetown University Press, 2001), 72.

3. Address given on the Laity's Role in the Church in France after the Separation of Church and State. Text in *L'avenir des travailleurs*, April 14, 1907; quoted in *Demain*, May 3, 1907, 445. Quoted in Yves Congar, *Lay People in the Church*, trans. Donald Attwater (London: Geoffrey Chapman, 1959), xxix.

4. Acts 15:22.

5. Acts 15:8.

6. Ephesians 4:4–6.

7. Jean-Pierre Jossua, OP, *Yves Congar: Theology in the Service of God's People* (Chicago: Priory Press, 1968), 58.

8. Timothy I. MacDonald, *The Ecclesiology of Yves Congar: Foundational Themes* (Lanham, MD: University Press of America, 1984), 238.

9. Christophe Potworowski, *Contemplation and Incarnation: The Theology of Marie-Dominique Chenu* (Montreal, Quebec, Canada: McGill-Queen's University Press, 2001), 161.

10. John Henry Newman, *On Consulting the Faithful in Matters of Doctrine*, 1859, ed. John Coulson (New York: Sheed and Ward, 1962, © 1961).

11. Avery Dulles, SJ, *Newman* (London and New York: Continuum, 2002), 106.

12. *Lumen Gentium* in *The Documents of Vatican II*, 11 July 2004, 12. Hereafter referred to as LG. Available online at http://www.vatican.va/archive/hist_councils/ii_vatican_council/documents/vat-ii_const_19641121_lumen-gentium_en.html.

13. Richard Lennan, *The Ecclesiology of Karl Rahner* (Oxford: Oxford University Press, 1995), 100.

14. Lennan, *Ecclesiology*, 105.

15. John Henry Newman, *Lectures on the Present Position of Catholics in England* (New York: America Press, 1942), 300.

16. Yves Congar, OP, *Power and Poverty in the Church*, trans. Jennifer Nicholson (Baltimore: Helicon, 1964), 65, 106, 109. [French original, 1953]

17. Dulles, *Newman*, 151.

18. B. C. Butler, OSB, "Newman and the Second Vatican Council," in *The Rediscovery of Newman: An Oxford Symposium*, eds. John Coulson and A. M. Allchin (London: SPCK, 1967), 235–46, at 242.

19. John H. Wright, "Modern Trends in Theological Method," in *Current Trends in Theology*, eds. Donald Wolf, SJ, and James Schall, SJ (Garden City, NY: Doubleday and Company, 1965), 32–57, at 41.

20. Arno Schilson, "The Major Theological Themes of Romano Guardini," in *Romano Guardini: Proclaiming the Sacred in a Modern World*, ed. Robert A. Krieg, CSC (Chicago: Liturgy Training Publications, 1995), 31–42, at 38.

21. M.-D. Chenu, OP, "The History of Salvation and the Historicity of Man in the Renewal of Theology," in *Theology of Renewal*, Vol. I, ed. L. K. Shook, CSB (Montreal: Palm Publishers, 1968), 153–66, at 157.

22. Potworowski, *Contemplation and Incarnation*, 95, 161, 189.

23. George Sim Johnston, "Open Windows: Why Vatican II Was Necessary," *Crisis Magazine*, March 9, 2004. Available at www.crisismagazine. com/march2004/Johnston/htm.

24. Pope Pius X, *Vehementer Nos*, ASS 39 (1906), 8–9.

25. Pope John Paul II, Exhortation, *Christifideles Laici* 25, "On the Vocation and the Mission of the Lay Faithful in the Church and the World" (Vatican City: Vatican City Press, 1988).

26. Pope Pius XII, *Documentation Catholique* 43 (1946), 146.

27. Leon Cardinal Joseph Suenens, *Memories and Hopes* (Dublin: Veritas Publications, 1992), 95.

28. LG 30.

29. LG 39.

30. LG 40.

31. LG 41.

32. LG 40.

33. MacDonald, *Ecclesiology of Yves Congar*, 265.

34. Ephesians 4:5.

35. Leon Cardinal Joseph Suenens, *Coresponsibility in the Church*, trans. Francis Martin (New York: Herder & Herder, 1968), 30.

36. LG 31.

37. LG 31.

38. LG 31.

39. LG 34.

40. LG 35.

41. LG 36.

42. LG 10.

43. Paul Lakeland, *The Liberation of the Laity* (New York: Continuum, 2002), 90.

44. LG 33.

45. LG 33.

46. LG 12.

47. Acts 15:22.

48. Richard McBrien, "The Church," in *Modern Catholicism: Vatican II and After*, ed. Adrian Hastings (New York: Oxford University Press, 1991), 84–95, at 93.

49. Dulles, *Newman*, 99.

50. LG 37.

51. LG 37.

52. LG 37.

53. LG 37.

54. Thomas Rausch, SJ, "A Theology of the Laity, and the Future of Ministry," *Tidings*, October 18, 2002. Available at http://www.the-tidings.com/2002/1018/rausch.htm.

55. Yves Congar, OP, "A Last Look at the Council," in *Vatican II Revisited by Those Who Were There*, ed. Dom Alberic Stacpoole, OSB (Minneapolis: Winston Press, 1986), 337–58, at 347.

56. Lakeland, *Liberation of the Laity*, 98.

57. GS 2.

58. Suenens, *Coresponsibility*, 210.

59. GS 43.

60. Schilson, "Major Themes of Romano Guardini," 34.

61. Samuel D. Femiano, *Infallibility of the Laity: The Legacy of Newman* (New York: Herder & Herder, 1967), 109.

62. Yves Congar, OP, *Laity, Church, and World*, trans. Donald Attwater (Baltimore: Helicon Press, 1960), 68. Italics his.

63. GS 62.

64. GS 43.

65. Giuseppe Alberigo and Joseph Komonchak, eds., *The History of Vatican II*, Vol. II (Maryknoll, NY: Orbis Books, 1970), 499.

66. Alberigo and Komonchak, *History of Vatican II*, Vol. II, 440–41.

67. Cardinal F. Cento, see *Relatio super Schema de Apostolatu Laicorum* (Vatican City: Typis Polyglottis Vaticanis, 1964), 4.

68. *Apostolicam Actuositatem* in *The Documents of Vatican II*, 11 July 2004, 1. Hereafter referred to as AA. Available online at http://www.vatican.va/archive/hist_councils/ii_vatican_council/documents/vat-ii_decree_19651118_apostolicam-actuositatem_en.html.

69. AA 5.

70. AA 25.

71. Lennan, *Ecclesiology*, 104–5.

72. Lennan, *Ecclesiology*, 107.

73. AA 23.

74. 1 Peter 3:15.

75. AA 6.

76. Yves Congar, OP, *Report from Rome: Second Session*, trans. Lancelot Sheppard (London: Geoffrey Chapman, Ltd., 1964), 79.

77. See comments of Edward Schillebeeckx in Lakeland, *Liberation of the Laity*, 108; Francine Cardman, "The Church Would Look Foolish without Them: Women and Laity since Vatican II," in *Vatican II: Open Questions and New Horizons*, ed. Gerald M. Fagin, SJ (Wilmington, DE: Michael Glazier, Inc., 1984), 105–33, at 110–11.

78. Yves Congar, OP, "Interview in Strasbourg, 1964," in *Trente ans de souvenirs*, a video produced by the Dominican Province in France. See *CTSA Proceedings* 59 (June 10–13, 2004), 162–66, at 163.

Chapter 4: The Church Looks at Itself

1. Michael A. Fahey, SJ, "Church," in *Systematic Theology: Roman Catholic Perspectives*, Vol. II, eds. Francis Schüssler Fiorenza and John P. Galvin (Minneapolis: Fortress Press, 1991), 3–74, at 31.

2. Thomas Bokenkotter, *A Concise History of the Catholic Church* (New York: Doubleday, 1990), 291.

3. *Pastor Aeternus*, c. 3; Eng. trans., *Decrees of the Ecumenical Councils*, 2 vols., ed. Norman Tanner, SJ (London and Washington, DC: Sheed & Ward and Georgetown University Press, 1990), 2:814.

4. Timothy G. McCarthy, *The Catholic Tradition* (Chicago: Loyola University Press, 1994), 2.

5. Thomas Rausch, SJ, *Catholicism at the Dawn of the Third Millennium* (Collegeville, MN: Liturgical Press, 1996), 1.

6. Bernard Lauret, ed., *Fifty Years of Catholic Theology: Conversations with Yves Congar*, trans. John Bowden (Philadelphia: Fortress Press, 1988), 40.

7. Lauret, *Fifty Years*, 43.

8. Richard Lennan, *The Ecclesiology of Karl Rahner* (Oxford: Clarendon Press, 1995), 142.

9. Lennan, *Ecclesiology*, 213.

10. Quoted in Lennan, *Ecclesiology*, 30, from Karl Rahner, "Thoughts on the Possibility of Belief Today," Theological Investigations v. 16 ("Uber

die Moglichkeit des Glaubens heute," Schriften zur Theologie v. 25). [orig. pub. 1962]

11. Lennan, *Ecclesiology*, 29.

12. Quoted in Lennan, *Ecclesiology*, 30, from Karl Rahner, "Belief Today."

13. Lennan, *Ecclesiology*, 135.

14. Giacomo Martina, SJ, "The Historical Context in Which the Idea of a New Ecumenical Council Was Born," in *Vatican II: Assessment and Perspectives*, Vol. I, ed. Rene Latourelle, SJ (Mahwah, NJ: Paulist Press, 1988), 3–73, at 13.

15. Quoted in Yves Congar, OP, "Moving toward a Pilgrim Church," in *Vatican II Revisited by Those Who Were There*, ed. Dom Alberic Stacpoole, OSB (Minneapolis: Winston Press, 1986), 129–152, at 130, from Antonio Acerbi's *Due ecclesiologie, Ecclesiologia giuridica ed Ecclesiologia di communione nella Lumen Gentium* (Bologna: Nuovi Saggi Teologici, 1975).

16. Richard P. McBrien, "The Church (*Lumen Gentium*)," in *Modern Catholicism: Vatican II and After*, ed. Adrian Hastings (New York: Oxford University Press, 1991), 84–95, at 85.

17. Cardinal Giovanni Montini, "Il mistero della chiesa nella luce di S. Ambrogio," in *L'Osservatore Romano* (December 10–11, 1962), 6.

18. Pope Paul VI, "Coronation Address," June 30, 1963.

19. Congar, "Pilgrim Church," in *Vatican II Revisited*, ed. Stacpoole, 129–52, at 134.

20. McBrien, "Church," 85, 88. It should be noted here that the *ad extra* discussion was later separated off in a document referred to as "schema 13." This document would ultimately be promulgated as *Gaudium et Spes*.

21. Pope Paul VI, "Opening Address," Second Session of Vatican II, September 29, 1963.

22. Michael Buckley, SJ, "Within the Holy Mystery," in *A World of Grace*, ed. Leo J. O'Donovan (New York: Crossroad, 1981), 31–49, at 40.

23. Michael G. Lawler and Thomas J. Shanahan, SJ, *Church: A Spirited Communion* (Collegeville, MN: Liturgical Press, 1995), 7.

24. *Acta Synodalia* 2/1:455.

25. Walter Kasper, *Theology and Church* (New York: Crossroad, 1989), 151.

26. Lawler and Shanahan, *Church*, 6.

27. Gerard Philips, "History of the Constitution," in *Commentary on the Documents of Vatican II*, Vol. I, ed. Herbert Vorgrimler (New York: Herder & Herder, 1967), 105–137, at 112.

28. *Lumen Gentium* 2, 3, 4. Hereafter referred to LG.

29. Henri de Lubac, SJ, *The Church: Paradox and Mystery*, trans. James R. Dunne (New York: Alba House, 1969), 14. [French orig. 1967]

30. Robert A. Krieg, CSC, *Romano Guardini: A Precursor of Vatican II* (Notre Dame, IN: University of Notre Dame Press, 1997), 57, 52, 58.

31. See Josef Meyer zu Schlochtern, *Sakrament Kirche* (Freiburg: Herder, 1992), 43–44; Avery Dulles, SJ, "Theology and Philosophy," in *The Craft of Theology*, exp. ed. (New York: Crossroad, 1995), 119–34, 120.

32. Dennis M. Doyle, *Communion Ecclesiology: Vision and Versions* (Maryknoll, NY: Orbis Books, 2000), 58.

33. Henri de Lubac, SJ, *Catholicism*, trans. L. C. Sheppard (London: Burns & Oates, 1950), 291.

34. LG 1, 48.

35. Lennan, *Ecclesiology*, 18.

36. Quoted in Lennan, *Ecclesiology*, 28, from Karl Rahner, SJ, "Confessions," *Theological Investigations* iii. 187 (*Schriften zur Theologie* iii. 223).

37. LG 8.

38. John W. O'Malley, SJ, "Development, Reforms, and Two Great Reformations: Towards a Historical Assessment of Vatican II," *Theological Studies* 44 (1983), 373–406, at 394.

39. Lennan, *Ecclesiology*, 81.

40. Karl Rahner, SJ, "Changing Church," in *The Christian of the Future*, trans. W. J. O'Hara (London: Burns & Oates, 1967), 36.

41. H. Bouillard, SJ, *Conversion et grace chez S. Thomas d'Aquin* (Paris: Aubier, Editions Montaigne, 1944), 219.

42. 1 Timothy 2:4.

43. Aloys Grillmeier, SJ "Mystery of the Church," in *Commentary on the Documents of Vatican II*, Vol. I, ed. Herbert Vorgrimler, trans. Kevin Smyth (New York: Herder & Herder, 1967), 138–52, at 140.

44. LG 16.

45. *Gaudium et Spes* 22. Hereafter referred to as GS.

46. John Galvin, "Salvation outside the Church," in *The Gift of the Church*, ed. Peter C. Phan (Collegeville, MN: Liturgical Press, 2000), 249–66, at 264.

47. Pope Paul VI, "Opening Address."

48. Hermann J. Pottmeyer, "A New Phase in the Reception of Vatican II: Twenty Years after the Council," in *The Reception of Vatican II*, eds. Giuseppe Alberigo, Jean-Pierre Jossua, OP, and Joseph Komonchak, trans. Matthew J. O'Connell (Washington, DC: Catholic University of America Press, 1987), 27–43, at 29. [French orig. 1985]. See also Doyle, *Communion*, 73, 78; Lawler and Shanahan, *Church*, 1; Cardinal Joseph Ratzinger, Congregation for the Doctrine of the Faith, *Catholic International* 3 (1992), 761, n. 1; Hermann J. Pottmeyer, "Dialogue as a Model for Communication in the Church," *Catholic International* (November 2001), 41–44; Joseph Komonchak, "The Significance of Vatican II for Ecclesiology," in *The Gift of the Church*, ed. Peter C. Phan (Collegeville, MN: Liturgical Press, 2000), 69–92, at 88; Patrick Granfield, *The Papacy in Transition* (Garden City, NY: Doubleday and Company, 1980), 60, 63; Krieg, *Romano Guardini*, 52, 66; Josef Franz van Beeck, SJ, *Catholic Identity after Vatican II* (Chicago: Loyola University Press, 1985), 39.

49. Doyle, *Communion*, 12, 13.

50. Miguel M. Garijo-Guembe, *Communion of Saints* (Collegeville, MN: Liturgical Press, 1994), 37, 2, xi.

51. LG 12.

52. Doyle, *Communion*, 48.

53. Fahey, "Church," 31.

54. Bradford E. Hinze, "The Holy Spirit and the Catholic Tradition," in *The Legacy of the Tübingen School*, eds. Donald J. Dietrich and Michael J. Himes (New York: Crossroad Publishing Company, 1977), 78.

55. Yves Congar, OP, "Johann Adam Mohler, 1796–1837," *Theologische Quartalschift* 150 (1970), 50–51, at 51.

56. Michael J. Himes, "The Development of Ecclesiology: Modernity to the Twentieth Century," in *The Gift of the Church*, ed. Peter C. Phan (Collegeville, MN: Liturgical Press, 2000), 45–67, at 58–59.

57. McBrien, "Church," 84.

58. Pottmeyer, "Dialogue," at 41–42.

59. Komonchak, "Significance of Vatican II," at 87.

60. LG 22.

61. Karl Rahner, SJ, "Chapter III—Articles 18–27," in *Commentary on the Documents of Vatican II*, Vol. I, ed. Herbert Vorgrimler (New York: Herder & Herder, 1967), 186–218, at 187.

62. Granfield, *Papacy in Transition*, 60.

63. Timothy I. MacDonald, *The Ecclesiology of Yves Congar: Foundational Themes* (Lanham, MD: University Press of America, 1984), 303.

64. Thomas F. O'Meara, OP, "Beyond 'Hierarchology,'" in *Legacy of the Tübingen School*, eds. Dietrich and Himes, 173–91, at 182.

65. Krieg, *Romano Guardini*, 63.

66. Patrick Granfield, *Theologians at Work* (New York: Macmillan Company, 1967), 256.

67. Granfield, *Papacy*, 63.

68. LG 26, 23.

69. Ephesians 4:5.

70. Yves Congar, OP, *I Believe in the Holy Spirit*, 3 vols., trans. David Smyth (New York: Seabury, 1983; Crossroad, 1997), 3:5.

71. Elizabeth Teresa Groppe, "The Contribution of Yves Congar's Theology of the Holy Spirit," *Theological Studies* 62 (2001), 451–78, at 463.

72. Pope John XXIII, *Ad Petri Cathedram*, AAS, t. LI, 1959, 513.

73. Yves Congar, OP, *A History of Theology*, trans. and ed. Hunter Guthrie, SJ (Garden City, NY: Doubleday and Company, 1968), 273.

74. Doyle, *Communion*, 75–76.

75. LG 27.

76. Gerald O'Collins, SJ, and Edward G. Farrugia, SJ, *A Concise Dictionary of Theology*, rev. and exp. (Mahwah, NJ: Paulist Press, 2000), 221.

77. Pottmeyer, "Dialogue," 42.

78. Yves Congar, OP, "Reception as an Ecclesiological Reality," in *Concilium*, English ed., no. 77, trans. John Griffiths (New York: Herder & Herder, 1972), 43–68, at 45.

79. Leon Joseph Cardinal Suenens, *Coresponsibility in the Church*, trans. Francis Martin (New York: Herder & Herder, 1968), 29.

80. LG 35, 37.

81. Gregory Baum, "Foreword," in *The New Agenda* by Andrew Greeley (Garden City, NY: Doubleday and Company, 1973), 11–34, at 14.

82. Michael J. Himes, "What Can We Learn from the Church in the Nineteenth Century?" in *The Church in the 21st Century*, ed. Michael J. Himes (Liguori, MO: Liguori Press, 2004), 65–69, at 66.

83. Brian Martin, *John Henry Newman: His Life and Work* (Mahwah, NJ: Paulist Press, 1990), 75.

84. LG 1. Italics mine.

85. Johann Sebastian von Drey, *Brief Introduction to the Study of Theology with Reference to the Scientific Standpoint and the Catholic System*,

trans. Michael J. Himes (Notre Dame, IN: University of Notre Dame Press, 1994), 117.

86. LG 5.

87. Lennan, *Ecclesiology*, 251.

88. O'Malley, "Developments," 392.

89. Giuseppe Alberigo, "Major Results, Shadows of Uncertainty," in *History of Vatican II*, Vol. IV, eds. Giuseppe Alberigo and Joseph Komonchak (Maryknoll, NY: Orbis Books, 2002), 617–48, at 624–25.

90. LG 9. Italics mine.

91. Yves Congar, OP, *La Vie Intellectuelle* 29 (1934), 247.

92. O'Collins and Farrugia, *Dictionary*, 79.

93. Walter Kasper, *The Methods of Dogmatic Theology*, trans. John Drury (New York: Paulist Press, 1969), 24.

94. Garijo-Guembe, *Communion*, 5–6.

95. LG 48.

96. Jean-Pierre Jossua, OP, *Yves Congar: Theology in the Service of God's People* (Chicago: Priory Press, 1968), 114.

97. Yves Congar, OP, "Theology's Task after Vatican II, " in *Theology of Renewal*, Vol. 1, ed. L. K. Schook, CSB (Montreal: Palm Publishers, 1968), 47–65, at 56.

98. MacDonald, *Ecclesiology*, 303.

99. Lennan, *Ecclesiology*, 74.

100. John Coulson, "Newman on the Church—His Final View, Its Origins and Influence," in *The Rediscovery of Newman: An Oxford Symposium*, eds. John Coulson and A. M. Allchin (London: SPCK, 1967), 123–43, at 133.

101. LG 8.

102. Quoted in Lennan, *Ecclesiology*, 152n61. Karl Rahner, "Was wurde erreicht?" in *Sind die Erwartungen erfullt?* eds. Karl Rahner, Oscar Cullman, and Heinrich Fries (Munich, 1966), 31.

103. LG 8.

104. Johann Adam Mohler, *Unity in the Church or the Principle of Catholicism Presented in the Spirit of the Church Fathers of the First Three Centuries*, ed. and trans. Peter C. Erb (Washington, DC: Catholic University of America Press, 1996), 9.

105. Karl Rahner, SJ, "The Development of Dogma," in *Theological Investigations*, Vol. I, trans. Cornelius Ernst, OP (Baltimore, MD: Helicon Press, 1963), 39–77, at 52.

106. Christophe Potworowski, *Contemplation and Incarnation: The Theology of Marie-Dominique Chenu* (Montreal, Quebec, Canada: McGill-Queen's University Press, 2001), 195.

107. LG 4, 9.

108. Lawler and Shanahan, *Church*, 5.

109. Joseph Komonchak, *CTSA Proceedings* 59 (June 10–13, 2004), 166.

110. Henri de Lubac, SJ, *The Discovery of God*, trans. Alexander Dru (Grand Rapids, MI: William B. Eerdmans Publishing Company, 1996), 177.

111. Lawler and Shanahan, *Church*, 2.

112. John W. O'Malley, SJ, "Interpreting Vatican II: Version Two," *Commonweal* 128:5 (March 9, 2001), 17.

113. John 16:13.

114. Matthew 28:19–20.

115. GS 43.

116. Jossua, *Yves Congar*, 161.

117. O'Meara, "Beyond 'Hierarchology,'" 177.

118. Quoted in Leon-Joseph Cardinal Suenens, *A New Pentecost?*, trans. Francis Martin (New York: Crossroad/Seabury Press, 1975), xi, from Blaise Pascal's *Pensees*, 14.

119. Martina, "Historical Context," 56.

120. Suenens, *A New Pentecost?*, 16.

Epilogue

1. Gregory Baum, "Interview," in *Voices from the Council*, eds. Michael Prendergast and M. D. Ridge (Portland, OR: Pastoral Press, 2004), 129–143, at 132.

2. Ladislas Orsy, SJ, "A Lesson in Ecclesiology," in *Vatican II: Forty Personal Stories*, eds. William Madges and Michael J. Daley (Mystic, CT: Twenty-Third Publications, 2003), 78–81, at 79.

3. Philip Paul Bliss, "The Ninety and Nine," Song and Quartet (1874).

4. Jean-Pierre Jossua, OP, *Yves Congar: Theology in the Service of God's People* (Chicago: Priory Press, 1968), 46.

5. Frans Jozef van Beeck, SJ, *Catholic Identity after Vatican II* (Chicago: Loyola University Press, 1985), 4.

6. Thomas F. O'Meara, OP, "A History of Grace," in *A World of Grace*, ed. Leo J. O'Donovan (New York: Crossroad, 1981), 76–91, at 77.

7. Jossua, *Yves Congar*, 182.

8. See also Letter of Pope Paul VI to the International Theological Congress of Rome, September 21, 1966; Giuseppe Alberigo, "Major Results, Shadows of Uncertainty," in *History of Vatican II*, Vol. IV (Maryknoll, NY: Orbis Books, 2002), 617–40, at 625; Leon Joseph Cardinal Suenens, *Coresponsibility in the Church*, trans. Francis Martin (New York: Herder & Herder, 1968), 29.

9. Alberic Stacpoole, OSB, "Introduction," in *Vatican II Revisited by Those Who Were There*, ed. Alberic Stacpoole, OSB (Minneapolis: Winston Press, 1986), 1–15, at 13.

10. Jossua, *Yves Congar*, 161.

11. John 14:26; 16:12.

12. John 16:12.

13. Jossua, *Yves Congar*, 182.

14. Karl Rahner, SJ, "The Council: A New Beginning," in *The Church after the Council* (New York: Herder & Herder, 1966), 9–33, at 19.

15. Leon Joseph Cardinal Suenens, *A New Pentecost?*, trans. Francis Martin (New York: Crossroad/Seabury Press, 1975), xiii.

BIBLIOGRAPHY

Abbott, Walter. *Twelve Council Fathers*. New York: The Macmillan Co., 1963.

Acerbi, Antonio. "Receiving Vatican II in a Changed Historical Context." *Concilium*, no. 186 (1981), 77–84.

———. *Due ecclesiologie: Ecclesiologia giuridica ed Ecclesiologia di communione nella Lumen Gentium*. Bologna: Nuovi Saggi Teologici, 1975.

Alberigo, Giuseppe, and Gustavo Gutierrez, eds. *Where Does the Church Stand?* English language ed. Marcus Lefebure. New York: Seabury Press, 1981.

Alberigo, Giuseppe, and Joseph Komonchak, eds. *History of Vatican II*. Four vols. Maryknoll, NY: Orbis; Leuven: Peeters, 1995–2003.

Alberigo, Giuseppe. "Major Results, Shadows of Uncertainty," in *History of Vatican II*, Vol. IV. Edited by Giuseppe Alberigo and Joseph Komonchak. Maryknoll, NY: Orbis Books, 2002, 617–48.

Apostolicam Actuositatem in *The Documents of Vatican II*, 11 July 2004. http://www.vatican.va/archive/hist_councils/ii_vatican_council/documents/vat-ii_decree_19651118_apostolicam-actuositatem_en.html.

Bacik, James. *Contemporary Theologians*. Chicago: Thomas More Press, 1989.

Baum, Gregory. "Foreword," in *The New Agenda*, by Andrew Greeley. Garden City, NY: Doubleday and Company, 1973, 11–34.

———. "Interview," in *Voices from the Council*. Edited by Michael Prendergast and M. D. Ridge. Portland, OR: Pastoral Press, 2004, 129–43.

Becker, Werner. "Newman's Influence in Germany," in *The Rediscovery of Newman: An Oxford Symposium.* Edited by John Coulson and A. M. Allchin. London: Sheed & Ward, 1967, 174–89.

Bellitto, Christopher. *The General Councils.* Mahwah, NJ: Paulist Press, 2002.

Bellitto, Christopher. *Renewing Christianity.* Mahwah, NJ: Paulist Press, 2001.

Benson, John E. "The History of the Historical-Critical Method in the Church: A Survey," *Dialog* 12 (1973), 94–103.

Bergant, Dianne, CSA. "Sacred Scripture: Light for Our Path." *Vatican II Today* (June 2004). Available at http://www.american catholic.org/Newsletters/VAT/aq0604.asp.

Bliss, Philip Paul. "The Ninety and Nine," Song and Quartet (1874).

Bokenkotter, Thomas. *A Concise History of the Catholic Church.* Revised and expanded edition. New York: Doubleday, 1990.

Borzaga, Reynold. *In Pursuit of Religion: A Framework for Understanding Today's Theology.* Palm Springs, FL: Sunday Publications, 1977.

Bouillard, H., SJ. *Conversation et grace chez S. Thomas d'Aquin.* Paris: Aubier, Editions Montaigne, 1944.

Bouyer, Louis. "The Permanent Relevance of Newman," in *Newman Today.* 1988 Proceedings of the Wethersfield Institute, Vol. I. Edited by Stanley L. Jaki. San Francisco: Ignatius Press, 1989, 165–74.

Buckley, Michael. "Within the Holy Mystery," in *A World of Grace.* Edited by Leo J. O'Donovan. New York: Crossroad, 1981, 31–49.

Burns, Robert, OP. *Roman Catholicism: Yesterday and Today.* Chicago: Loyola University Press, 1992.

———. *Roman Catholicism after Vatican II.* Washington, DC: Georgetown University Press, 2001.

Butler, B. C., OSB. "Newman and the Second Vatican Council," in *The Rediscovery of Newman: An Oxford Symposium.* Edited by John Coulson and A. M. Allchin. London: SPCK, 1967, 235–46.

Butler, Christopher. *The Theology of Vatican II.* Westminster, MD: Christian Classics, Inc., 1981.

Byrne, Brendan, SJ. "Scripture and Vatican II: A Very Incomplete Journey," *Compass* 38 (Winter 2003). Available at http://www.compassreview.org/winter03/2.html.

Cardman, Francine. "The Church Would Look Foolish without Them: Women and Laity since Vatican II," in *Vatican II: Open Questions and New Horizons.* Edited by Gerald M. Fagin, SJ (Wilmington, DE: Michael Glazier, Inc., 1984), 105–33.

Chenu, Marie-Dominique, OP. "The History of Salvation and the Historicity of Man in the Renewal of Theology," in *Theology of Renewal*, Vol. I. Edited by L. K. Schook, CSB. Montreal: Palm Publishers, 1968, 153–66.

Congar, Yves, OP. *Dialogue between Christians: Catholic Contributions to Ecumenism.* Translated by Philip Loretz, SJ. Westminster, MD: Newman Press, 1966.

———. *Diversity and Communion.* Translated by John Bowden. London: SCM Press Ltd., 1984.

———. *Divided Christendom: A Catholic Study of the Problem of Reunion.* London: G. Bles, 1939. [English translation]

———. *Eglise et Papante.* Paris: Editions du Cerf, 1994.

———. *A History of Theology.* Translated and edited by Hunter Guthrie. Garden City, NY: Doubleday, 1968.

———. *I Believe in the Holy Spirit.* Three vols. Translated by David Smith. New York: Seabury Press, 1983; Crossroad, 1997.

———. "Interview in Strasbourg, 1964," in *Trente ans de souvenirs.* A video produced by the Dominic Province in France. See CTSA *Proceedings*, 59 (June 10–13, 2004), 162–66.

———. "Johann Adam Mohler, 1796–1837," in *Theologische Quartalschift* 150 (1970), 50–51.

———. *Laity, Church, and World.* Baltimore: Helicon Press, 1960.

———. "A Last Look at the Council," in *Vatican II Revisited by Those Who Were There.* Edited by Dom Alberic Stacpoole, OSB. Minneapolis: Winston Press, 1986, 337–58.

———. *Laypeople in the Church.* Translated by Donald Attwater. London: Geoffrey Chapman, 1959.

———. "Moving toward a Pilgrim Church," in *Vatican II Revisited by Those Who Were There.* Edited by Dom Alberic Stacpoole, OSB. Minneapolis: Winston Press, 1986, 129–52.

———. *Power and Poverty in the Church*. Translated by Jennifer Nicholson. Baltimore. Helicon, 1964. [French original 1953]

———. "Reception as an Ecclesiological Reality," *Concilium*, no. 77. Translated by John Griffiths. New York: Herder & Herder, 1972, 43–68. [English edition]

———. *Report from Rome: First Session*. Translated by A. Manson. London: Geoffrey Chapman Ltd., 1963.

———. *Report from Rome: Second Session*. Translated by Lancelot Sheppard. London: Geoffrey Chapman, Ltd., 1964.

———. "Theology's Tasks after Vatican II," in *Theology of Renewal*, Vol. I. Edited by L. K. Shook, CSB. Montreal: Palm Publishers, 1968, 47–65.

———. *This Church That I Love*. Translated by Lucien Delafuente. New Jersey: Dimension Books, 1969.

———. *La Vie Intellectuelle* 29 (1934).

———. *Vraie et Fausse Reforme dans l'Eglise*. Paris: Editions du Cerf, 1950.

Connolly, James M. *The Voices of France*. New York: Macmillan Company, 1961.

Coulson, John, and A. M. Allchin, eds. *The Rediscovery of Newman: An Oxford Symposium*. London: SPCK, 1967.

Coulson, John. "Newman on the Church – his final view, its origins and influence," in *The Rediscovery of Newman: An Oxford Symposium*. Edited by John Coulson and A. M. Allchin. London: SPCK, 1967, 123–43.

Crichton, J. D. *Light in the Darkness: Forerunners of the Liturgical Movement*. Collegeville, MN: Liturgical Press, 1996.

de Lubac, Henri, SJ. *Catholicism*. Translated by L. C. Sheppard. London: Burns & Oates, 1950.

———. *The Church: Paradox and Mystery*. Translated by James R. Dunne. New York: Alba House, 1969. [French original 1967]

———. *The Discovery of God*. Translated by Alexander Dru. Grand Rapids, MI: William B. Eerdmans Publishing Company, 1996.

Dessain, Charles Stephen. *John Henry Newman*. London: Thomas Nelson & Sons, 1966.

Dibelius, Otto. *Das Jahrhundert der Kirche*. Second edition. Berlin: Furche, 1927.

DiDomizio, Daniel. "Jan Hus' *De Ecclesia*, Precursor of Vatican II?" *Theological Studies* 60 (1999), 247–60.

Dolan, Jay P. *The American Catholic Experience*. Garden City, NY: Doubleday, 1985.

Doyle, Dennis. *The Church Emerging from Vatican II*. Mystic, CT: Twenty-Third Publications, 1992.

———. *Communion Ecclesiology: Vision and Versions*. Maryknoll, NY: Orbis Books, 2000.

———. "Different Schools of Reform Led to Vatican II." Address given October 31, 1997, at the University of Dayton.

———. "Journet, Congar and the Roots of Communion Ecclesiology," *Theological Studies* 58 (September 1997), 461–80.

Dulles, Avery, SJ. "A Half Century of Ecclesiology," *Theological Studies* 50 (1989), 419–42.

———. *Newman*. London and New York: Continuum, 2002.

———. "Theology and Philosophy," in *The Craft of Theology*. Expanded edition. New York: Crossroad, 1995, 119–34.

Dych, William V. "Theology in a New Key," in *A World of Grace*. Edited by Leo J. O'Donovan. New York: Crossroad, 1981, 1–16.

Fagin, Gerald, ed. *Vatican II: Open Questions and New Horizons*. Wilmington, DE: Michael Glazier, Inc., 1984.

Fahey, Michael, SJ. "Church," in *Systematic Theology: Roman Catholic Perspectives*, Vol. II. Edited by Francis Schüssler Fiorenza and John P. Galvin. Minneapolis: Fortress Press, 1991, 1–74.

Femiano, Samuel. *Infallibility of the Laity: The Legacy of Newman*. New York: Herder & Herder, 1967.

Fernando, Bishop Frank Marcus. "Interview," in *Voices from the Council*. Edited by Michael Prendergast and M. D. Ridge. Portland, OR: Pastoral Press, 2004, 17–24.

Flannery, Austin, ed. *Vatican Council II: The Conciliar and Post-Conciliar Documents*, Vol. I. Northport, NY: Costello Publishing Co., 1998.

Fraccia, Charles A. *Second Spring: The Coming of Age of U.S. Catholicism*. San Francisco: Harper & Row, 1980.

Franklin, W. R. "The Nineteenth Century Liturgical Movement," *Worship* 53 (1979), 12–39.

Gallagher, John. *Time Past, Time Future: An Historical Study of Catholic Moral Theology*. Mahwah, NJ: Paulist Press, 1990.

Galvin, John P. "The Invitation of Grace," in *A World of Grace*. Edited by Leo J. O'Donovan. New York: Crossroad, 1981, 64–75.

———. "Salvation outside the Church," in *The Gift of the Church*. Edited by Peter C. Phan. Collegeville, MN: Liturgical Press, 2000, 249–66.

Garijo-Guembe, Miguel M. *Communion of Saints*. Collegeville, MN: Liturgical Press, 1994.

Gaudium et Spes in *The Documents of Vatican II*, 11 July 2004. http://www.vatican.va/archive.va/archive.hist_councils/ ii_vatican_council/documents/vat-ii_const_19651207_gaudium-et-spes_en.html.

Granfield, Patrick. "The Church as Institution: A Reformulated Model," *Journal of Ecumenical Studies* 16 (Summer 1979), 425–47.

———. *The Papacy in Transition*. Garden City, NY: Doubleday and Company, 1980.

———. *Theologians at Work*. New York: Macmillan Company, 1967.

Grillmeier, Aloys, SJ. "Mystery of the Church." Translated by Kevin Smyth in *Commentary on the Documents of Vatican II*, Vol. I. Edited by Herbert Vorgrimler. New York: Herder & Herder, 1967, 138–52.

Groppe, Elizabeth Teresa. "The Contribution of Yves Congar's Theology of the Holy Spirit," *Theological Studies* 62 (2001), 451–78.

Guardini, Romano. *Das Wesen des Christentums*. Wurzburg: Echter, 1938. [This text first appeared in 1929]

Gula, Richard. *Reason Informed by Faith: Foundations of Catholic Morality*. Mahwah, NJ: Paulist Press, 1989.

Hales, E. E. Y. *The Catholic Church in the Modern World*. Garden City, NY: Hanover House, 1958.

Hastings, Adrian. "Catholic History from Vatican I to John Paul II," in *Modern Catholicism: Vatican II and After*. Edited by Adrian Hastings. New York: Oxford University Press, 1991, 1–13.

Hastings, Adrian, ed. *Modern Catholicism: Vatican II and After*. New York: Oxford University Press, 1991.

Hebblethwaite, Peter. *John XXIII: Pope of the Century*. Revised edition by Margaret Hebblethwaite. New York: Continuum, 2000.

Hellwig, Monica. "Foundations for Theology," in *Faithful Witness*. Edited by Leo J. O'Donovan and T. Howland Sanks. New York: Crossroad Publishing Company, 1989, 1–13.

Himes, Michael. "The Development of Ecclesiology: Modernity to the Twentieth Century," in *Gift of the Church*. Edited by Peter C. Phan. Collegeville, MN: Liturgical Press, 2000, 45–67.

———. *Ongoing Incarnation: Johann Adam Mohler and the Beginnings of Modern Ecclesiology*. New York: Crossroad Publishing, 1997.

———. "What Can We Learn from the Church in the Nineteenth Century?" in *The Church in the 21st Century*. Edited by Michael J. Himes. Liguori, MO: Liguori Press, 2004, 65–79.

Hinze, Bradford E. "The Holy Spirit and the Catholic Tradition," in *The Legacy of the Tübingen School*. Edited by Donald J. Dietrich and Michael J. Himes. New York: Crossroad Publishing Company, 1977, 75–94.

"How Vatican II Turned the Church toward the World," *Time*, December 17, 1965, 24–25.

Jay, Eric. *The Church: Its Changing Image through Twenty Centuries*. Atlanta: John Knox, 1980.

Johnston, George Sim. "Open Windows: Why Vatican II Was Necessary," *Crisis*, March 9, 2004. Available at http://www.crisismagazine.com/march2004/johnston.htm.

Jossua, Jean-Pierre, OP. *Yves Congar: Theology in the Service of God's People*. Chicago: Priory Press, 1968.

Kasper, Walter. *Jesus the Christ*. Translated by V. Green. New York: Paulist Press, 1976.

———. *The Methods of Dogmatic Theology*. Translated by John Drury. New York: Paulist Press, 1969.

———. *Theology and Church*. New York: Crossroad, 1989.

Kelly, Geoffrey B., ed. *Karl Rahner: Theologian of the Graced Search for Meaning*. Minneapolis: Fortress Press, 1992.

Ker, Ian T. "Newman and the Postconciliar Church," in *Newman Today*. 1988 Proceedings of the Wethersfield Institute, Vol. 1. San Francisco: Ignatius Press, 1989, 121–41.

Ker, Ian, and Thomas Gornall, eds. *The Letters and Diaries of John Henry Newman*. Oxford: Clarendon Press, 1979.

Kilmartin, Edward. *Christian Liturgy*. Kansas City, MO: Sheed & Ward, 1988.

Koenker, E. B. *The Liturgical Renaissance in the Roman Catholic Church*. Chicago: University of Chicago Press, 1954. [Second edition, St. Louis, 1966]

Komonchak, Joseph. *CTSA Proceedings* 59 (June 10–13, 2004), 162–66.

———, ed. *History of Vatican II*, Vol. I. English version. Maryknoll, NY: Orbis Books, 1995.

———. "Return from Exile: Catholic Theology in the 1930s," in *The Twentieth Century: A Theological Overview*. Edited by Gregory Baum. Maryknoll, NY: Orbis Books, 1999, 35–48.

———. "The Significance of Vatican II for Ecclesiology," in *The Gift of the Church*. Edited by Peter C. Phan. Collegeville, MN: Liturgical Press, 2000, 69–92.

———. "Theology and Culture at Mid-Century: The Example of Henri de Lubac," *Theological Studies* 51:4 (December 1990), 579–610.

———. "Vatican II as Ecumenical Council: Yves Congar's Vision Realized," *Commonweal* 129:20 (November 22, 2002), 12.

Krieg, Robert A., CSC. "A Precursor's Life and Work," in *Romano Guardini: Proclaiming the Sacred in a Modern World*. Edited by Robert A. Krieg, CSC. Chicago: Liturgy Training Publication, 1995, 47–65.

———. *Romano Guardini: A Precursor of Vatican II*. Notre Dame, IN: University of Notre Dame Press, 1997.

Kung, Hans. *The Church*. Edited by Ray and Rosaleen Ockenden. New York: Sheed & Ward, 1967.

———. *The Council, Reform and Reunion*. Translated by Cecily Hastings. New York: Sheed & Ward, 1961.

Lakeland, Paul. *The Liberation of the Laity*. New York: Continuum, 2002.

Lane, Dermot. *Experience, God and Theology*. New York: Paulist Press, 1981.

Lauret, Bernard, ed. *Fifty Years of Catholic Theology: Conversations with Yves Congar*. Translated by John Bowden. Philadelphia: Fortress Press, 1988.

Lawler, Michael G., and Thomas J. Shanahan, SJ. *Church: A Spirited Communion*. Collegeville, MN: Liturgical Press, 1995.

Leger, Cardinal Paul-Emile. "Introduction," in *Theology of Renewal*, Vol. I. Edited by L. K. Schook, CSB. Montreal: Palm Publishers, 1968, 19–33.

Lennan, Richard. *The Ecclesiology of Karl Rahner.* Oxford: Oxford University Press, 1995.

Lindbeck, George. *The Future of Roman Catholic Theology: Vatican II— Catalyst for Change.* Philadelphia: Fortress Press, 1970.

Livingston, James C. *Modern Christian Thought: From the Enlightenment to Vatican II.* New Jersey: Prentice-Hall, 1971.

Lucker, Raymond, and William McDonough, eds. *Revelation and the Church.* Maryknoll, NY: Orbis Books, 2003.

Lumen Gentium in *The Documents of Vatican II*, 11 July 2004. http://www.vatican.va/archive/hist_councils/ii_vatican_council/ documents/vat-ii_const_19641121_lumen-gentium_en.html.

MacDonald, Timothy I. *The Ecclesiology of Yves Congar: Foundational Themes.* Lanham, MD: University Press of America, 1984.

Martin, Brian. *John Henry Newman: His Life and Work.* Mahwah, NJ: Paulist Press, 1990.

Martina, Giacomo, SJ. "The Historical Context in Which the Idea of a New Ecumenical Council Was Born." Translated by Leslie Wearne in *Vatican II: Assessment and Perspectives*, Vol. I. Edited by Rene Latourelle, SJ. Mahwah, NJ: Paulist Press, 1988, 3–73.

Martos, Joseph. *The Catholic Sacraments.* Wilmington, DE: Michael Glazier, Inc., 1983.

McBrien, Richard. "The Church (*Lumen Gentium*)," in *Modern Catholicism: Vatican II and After.* Edited by Adrian Hastings. New York: Oxford University Press, 1991, 84–95.

———. *Do We Need the Church?* New York: Harper & Row, 1969.

———. *Lives of the Popes.* San Francisco: Harper Collins, 1997.

McCarthy, Timothy. *The Catholic Tradition: Before and after Vatican II 1878*–1993. Chicago: Loyola University Press, 1994.

McCormick, Richard. *The Critical Calling: Reflections on Moral Dilemmas since Vatican II.* Washington, DC: Georgetown University Press, 1989.

Mersch, Emile. *The Whole Christ.* Milwaukee: Bruce, 1938. [English translation]

Metzger, Marcel. *History of the Liturgy: The Major Stages.* Collegeville, MN: Liturgical Press, 1999.

Misner, Paul. "Romano Guardini," in *New Catholic Encyclopedia*, Vol. 6. Second edition. Detroit, MI: Thomas/Gale; Washington, DC: Catholic University of America, 2003.

Mohler, Johann Adam. *Unity in the Church or the Principle of Catholicism Presented in the Spirit of the Church Fathers of the First Three Centuries.* Edited and translated by Peter C. Erb. Washington, DC: The Catholic University of America Press, 1966.

Montini, Giovani Battista. "Il mistero della chiesa nella luce di S. Ambrogio," *L'Osservatore Romano* (December 10–11, 1962).

New Catholic Encyclopedia. Second edition. Detroit, MI: Thomas/Gale; Washington, DC: Catholic University of America, 2003.

Newman, Cardinal John Henry. *An Essay on the Development of Doctrine, 1878* (Notre Dame, IN: University of Notre Dame Press, 1989).

———. *The Letters and Diaries of John Henry Newman,* Vol. XIX. Edited at the Birmingham Oratory with notes and an introduction by Ian Kerr and Thomas Gornall. Oxford: Clarendon Press, 1978.

———. *Letters and Diaries.* Vol. XXV.

———. *Letters on the Present Position of Catholics in England.* New York: America Press, 1942.

———. *On Consulting the Faithful in Matters of Doctrine,* 1859.

Nichols, Aidan. *From Newman to Congar.* Edinburgh: T & T Clark, 1990.

———. *The Shape of Catholic Theology.* Collegeville, MN: Liturgical Press, 1991.

Nugent, Robert, SDS. "Yves Congar: Apostle of Patience." *Australian EJournal of Theology,* no. 4 (February 2005). Available at http://dlibrary.acu.edu.au/research/theology/ejournal/aejt_4/nugent.htm.

O'Collins, Gerald, SJ, and Edward G. Farrugia, SJ. *A Concise Dictionary of Theology.* Mahwah, NJ: Paulist Press, 2000.

O'Connell, Timothy. "Vatican II: Setting, Themes, Future Agenda," in *Vatican II and Its Documents: An American Appraisal.* Edited by

Timothy O'Connell. Wilmington, DE: Michael Glazier, 1986, 237–55.

O'Donahue, N. D. "Vatican II: The Hidden Questions," *Doctrine and Life* 33 (1983), 41–47.

O'Donovan, Leo J. "In Memoriam: Karl Rahner, SJ, 1904–1984," *Journal of the American Academy of Religion* 53:1 (March 1985), 129–31.

O'Hanlon, Daniel. "Concluding Reflections," in *Current Trends in Theology*. Edited by Donald Wolf, SJ, and James Schall, SJ. Garden City, NY: Doubleday and Company, 1965, 271–77.

O'Malley, John, SJ. "Developments, Reforms, and Two Great Reformations: Toward a Historical Assessment of Vatican II," *Theological Studies* 44 (1983), 373–406.

———. "Interpreting Vatican II: Version Two," *Commonweal* 128:5 (March 9, 2001), 17.

———. "Reform, Historical Consciousness and Vatican II's *Aggiornamento*," *Theological Studies* 32 (1971), 573–601.

O'Meara, Thomas F., OP. Beyond 'Hierarchology,'" in *The Legacy of the Tübingen School*. New York: Crossroad Publishing Company, 1997, 173–91.

———. "A History of Grace," in *A World of Grace*. Edited by Leo J. O'Donovan. New York: Crossroad, 1981, 76–91.

———. "The Origins of the Liturgical Movement and German Romanticism," *Worship* 59 (1985), 326–53.

Orsy, Ladislas, SJ. *The Church: Learning and Teaching*. Wilmington, DE: Michael Glazier, Inc., 1987.

———. "A Lesson in Ecclesiology," in *Vatican II: Forty Personal Stories*. Edited by William Madges and Michael J. Daley. Mystic, CT: Twenty-Third Publications, 2003, 78–81.

Pascal, Blaise. *Pensees*. Paris: Librairie Garnier Freres, 14.

Pastor Aeternus, c. 3; English translation, *Decrees of the Ecumenical Councils*. Two vols. Edited by Norman P. Tanner, SJ. London and Washington, DC: Sheed & Ward and Georgetown University Press, 1990.

Pecklers, Keith. *The Unread Vision: The Liturgical Movement in the United States of America, 1926–1955*. Collegeville, MN: Liturgical Press, 1998.

Pelikan, Jaroslav. *The Christian Tradition: Christian Doctrine and Modern Culture since 1700*, Vol. 5. Chicago: University of Chicago Press, 1989.

Philips, Gerard. "History of the Constitution," in *Commentary on the Documents of Vatican II*, Vol. I. Edited by Herbert Vorgrimler. New York: Herder & Herder, 1967, 105–37.

———. *Le role du laicat dans l'eglise*. Paris: Casterman, 1954. [English translation Notre Dame, IN: Fides, 1956]

Pope John XXIII. "Opening Address of the Second Vatican Council." October 11, 1962.

———. *Pacem in Terris*, in *The Papal Encyclicals* 1958–1981. Edited by Claudia Carlen, IHM. Raleigh, NC: Pierian Press, 1990, 107–129.

———. *Ad Petri Cathedram*, AAS, t. LI, 1959.

Pope John Paul II. *Christifideles Laici 25. On the Vocation and the Mission of the Lay Faithful in the Church and the World*. Vatican City: Vatican City Press, 1988.

Pope Paul VI. "Coronation Address." June 30, 1963.

———. "Opening Speech." Second Session of Vatican II, September 29, 1963.

———. *L'Osservatore Romano*. Italian language edition, April 7–8, 1975.

Pope Pius X. *Vehementer Nos* ASS 39 (1906).

Pope Pius XII. *Divino Afflante Spiritu*, in *The Papal Encyclicals 1939–1958*. Edited by Claudia Carlen, IHM. Raleigh, NC: Pierian Press, 1990, 65–79.

———. *Documention Catholique* 43 (1946).

Pottmeyer, Hermann J. "Dialogue as a Model for Communication in the Church," *Catholic International* (November 2001), 41–44.

———. "A New Phase in the Reception of Vatican II: Twenty Years after the Council." Translated by Matthew J. O'Connell in *The Reception of Vatican II*. Edited by Giuseppe Alberigo, Jean-Pierre Jossua, OP, and Joseph Komonchak. Washington, DC: Catholic University of America Press, 1987. [French original 1985, 27–43]

Potworowski, Christophe. *Contemplation and Incarnation: The Theology of Marie-Dominique Chenu*. Montreal, Quebec, Canada: McGill-Queen's University Press, 2001.

Quinn, Edward. "Renewal of Theology," *Downside Review* 74 (October 1956), 289–301.

Quinn, John R. *The Reform of the Papacy.* New York: Crossroad Publishing Company, 1999.

Rahner, Karl, SJ. "Chapter III—Articles 18–27," in *Commentary on the Documents of Vatican II,* Vol. I. Edited by Herbert Vorgrimler. New York: Herder & Herder, 1967, 186–218.

———. *The Christian of the Future.* London: Burns & Oates, 1967.

———. *The Church and the Sacraments.* New York: Herder & Herder, 1963. [English translation]

———. "Concerning Vatican Council II," in *Theological Investigations,* Vol. VI. Translated by Karl-H. and Boniface Kruger. Baltimore: Helicon Press, 1969.

———. "Confessions, in *Theological Investigations.* iii. 187 (*Schriften zur Theologie* iii.223). Quoted in *The Ecclesiology of Karl Rahner,* Richard Lennan. Oxford: Oxford University Press, 1995, 152.

———. "The Council: A New Beginning," in *The Church after the Council.* New York: Herder & Herder, 1966, 9–33.

———. "The Development of Dogma," in *Theological Investigations,* Vol. I. Translated by Cornelius Ernst, OP. Baltimore: Helicon Press, 1963, 39–77.

———. *Foundations of Christian Faith: An Introduction to the Idea of Christianity.* Translated by William V. Dych. New York: Crossroad/Seabury Press, 1982.

———. "Notes on the Lay Apostolate," in *Theological Investigations* 2. Baltimore: Helicon, 1963, 319–52.

———. "Thoughts on the Possibility of Belief Today," *Theological Investigations* 16 ("Uber die Moglichkeit des Glaubens heute," Schriften zur Theologie 25). [Original publication 1962]

———. "Toward a Fundamental Theological Interpretation of Vatican II," *Theological Studies* 40 (1979), 716–27.

———. "Was wurde erreicht?" in *Sind die Erwartungen erfullt?* Edited by Karl Rahner, Oscar Cullman, and Heinrich Fries. Munich, 1966.

Ratzinger, Joseph Cardinal. Congregation for the Doctrine of the Faith, *Catholic International* 3 (1992).

———. *The Theological Highlights of Vatican II.* Mahwah, NJ: Paulist Press, 1966.

Ratzinger, Joseph, and Vittorio Messori. *The Ratzinger Report: An Exclusive Interview on the State of the Church.* San Francisco: Ignatius Press, 1985.

Rausch, Thomas, SJ. *Catholicism at the Dawn of the Third Millennium.* Collegeville, MN: Liturgical Press, 1996.

———. "A Theology of the Laity, and the Future of Ministry," *Tidings*, October 18, 2002. Available at http://www.the-tidings .com//2002/1018/rausch.htm.

Rosmini, Antonio. *The Five Wounds of the Church.* London: Rivingtons, 1883.

Schillebeeckx, Edward. *The Real Achievement of Vatican II.* New York: Herder & Herder, 1967.

Schilson, Arno. "The Major Theological Themes of Romano Guardini," in *Romano Guardini: Proclaiming the Sacred in a Modern World.* Edited by Robert A. Krieg, CSC. Chicago: Liturgy Training Publications, 1995), 31–42.

Schoof, T. M. *A Survey of Catholic Theology, 1800–1970.* Translated by N. D. Smith. Glen Rock, NJ: Paulist Newman Press, 1970.

Schreiter, Robert. "The Paradox of Vatican II: Theology in a New Millennium." Address given April 14, 2002, at the Bernadin Center at Catholic Theological Union.

Semmelroth, Otto. *Die Kirche als Ursakrament.* Frankfurt: Knecht, 1953.

Stacpoole, Alberic, OSB. "Introduction," in *Vatican II Revisited by Those Who Were There.* Edited by Alberic Stacpoole, OSB. Minneapolis: Winston Press, 1986, 1–15.

Stacpoole, Alberic, ed. *Vatican II Revisited by Those Who Were There.* Minneapolis: Winston Press, 1986.

Stahel, Thomas H. "Structures for the Vision: An Interview with Ladislas Orsy," *America* 173:10 (October 7, 1995), 10–15.

Suenens, Leon Joseph Cardinal. *The Church in Dialogue.* Edited by Arthur McCormack, MHM. Notre Dame, IN: Fides Publishers, Inc., 1965.

———. *Coresponsibility in the Church.* Translated by Francis Martin. New York: Herder & Herder, 1968.

———. *Memories and Hopes.* Dublin: Veritas Publications, 1992.

———. *A New Pentecost?* Translated by Francis Martin. New York: Seabury Press, 1975.

Sugrue, Francis. *Popes in the Modern World*. New York: Thomas Y. Crowell, Company, 1961.

Swidler, Leonard. *Toward a Catholic Constitution*. New York: Crossroad Publishing Company, 1966.

Synod of Bishops. "The Final Report," *Origins* 15:27 (December 19, 1985), 440–50.

van Beeck, Josef Franz, SJ. *Catholic Identity after Vatican II*. Chicago: Loyola University Press, 1985.

Vatican Council I. *Dogmatic Constitution on the Church*, in Decrees of the Ecumenical Councils, 2; Trent-Vatican II. Edited by Norman Tanner, SJ, 811–16.

von Drey, Johann Sebastian. *Brief Introduction to the Study of Theology with Reference to the Scientific Standpoint and the Catholic System*. Translated by Michael J. Himes. Notre Dame, IN: University of Notre Dame Press, 1994.

Vorgrimler, Herbert, ed. *Commentary on the Documents of Vatican II*, Vols. I–V. New York: Herder & Herder, 1967–1969.

Weger, Karl-Heinz. *Karl Rahner: An Introduction to His Theology*. New York: Crossroad/Seabury Press, 1980.

Willebrands, J. "Vatican II's Ecclesiology of Communion," *One in Christ* 23 (1987), 179–91.

Wiltgen, Ralph. *The Rhine Flows into the Tiber*. Rockford, IL: Tan Books and Publishers, Inc., 1967.

Wright, John H. "Modern Trends in Theological Method," in *Current Trends in Theology*. Edited by Donald Wolf, SJ, and James Schall, SJ. Garden City, NY: Doubleday and Company, 1965, 32–57.

INDEX